Interpreting the Bible

a handbook of Biblical understanding

Wilfred Kuhrt

GRACE PUBLICATIONS

GRACE PUBLICATIONS TRUST
139 Grosvenor Avenue
London
N5 2NH
England

General Editors:

H.J. Appleby
J.P. Arthur M.A.

© W. N. H. Kuhrt 1982
First published 1982
Second edition 1991

ISBN 0 95054 768 9

Distributed by:
EVANGELICAL PRESS
12 Wooler Street
Darlington
Co. Durham
DL1 1RQ
England

Typeset in Great Britain by Inset, Hertford Heath
Printed in Great Britain by Cox & Wyman, Reading

Dedicated to the memory of

James Willoughby

and

Norton Sterrett

Contents

Preface to the first edition (1982)

Although, at the time, there was no thought of writing a book, this little volume began to take shape more than thirty years ago when I prepared a chaotic sheaf of notes in mingled Tamil and English for the twenty students (men and women) whom I was privileged to teach for two years in Paniadipatti, Tamilnadu, South India. Twenty years later I was invited to give a series of lectures on Principles of Interpretation to the Staff Workers of the Union of Evangelical Students of India. So the now decaying sheaf of notes was resurrected, translated back into English, revised and reshaped. The Staff Workers of U.E.S.I. came from all over India but there were several of them who belonged to the Tamil Country and they began to show great interest when they learned that most of the material I was sharing with them had had a previous existence in their mother tongue. Eventually they suggested that I put it all back again into Tamil and prepare it for publication. This was done but it still had not been published by the time my wife and I were compelled by my ill health to leave India early in 1975. However, with the assistance of the Strict Baptist Mission and with the help and persistence of Olive Knight in India this little 76 page Tamil book was published by the Tamilnadu Evangelical Graduates' Fellowship in 1977.

Here, in London, in 1978/79 unexpected and welcome opportunities have arisen for conducting study classes for small groups of students on Bible Interpretation and Background. When it was noised abroad that I had written a book in Tamil on these subjects it was suggested that I should once again translate the material back into English with a view to publication in this country. And so the present book has emerged. It is not a mere translation of the Tamil book. Opportunity has been taken to make extensive revision and to add new material.

In the preparation of this book I must particularly acknowledge the inspiration and help afforded me by Bob Sheehan and Stephen Dray who in the midst of very busy pastoral responsibilities have read through my typescript and made many valuable suggestions. Mrs Steven Richards (Farnham), to whom we are greatly indebted, typed and retyped my terribly mangled document.

Preface to the second edition

It is with some surprise and much pleasure that I find myself called upon to prepare a second edition of this book at a time when the Tamil original has just appeared in a third edition. I am profoundly grateful to God and to the many who have encouraged me and taught me over the years.

An index kindly prepared by Jack E. Simmons has been added to this volume and also a brief chapter about the role of the Holy Spirit in our task of understanding and interpreting the Scriptures. I am indebted to Austin Walker (Crawley) who drew my attention to this gap in my first edition.

Although exposed, like everybody else in recent years, to many new and sometimes bewildering winds of hermeneutical change, I see no reason for making much change in my material and so the book issued in 1982 remains substantially the same in 1990.

I am glad that John Appleby (acting for Grace Publications) is to be responsible for seeing this second edition through the press because it gives me the opportunity to acknowledge gratefully a friendship and partnership which has endured since he joined us in Madras nearly 40 years ago. I must not forget also to pay tribute to my wife, Doris, whose tolerant loyalty for more than half a century has permitted me to read and read, almost to my heart's content, and to do a little writing as well.

W. H. Kuhrt, July 1990

1.
Foundation truths

It goes without saying that a good Christian worker must be thoroughly familiar with the Bible. He is to be a "teacher of the law . . . instructed about the kingdom of heaven" and "like the owner of a house, who brings out of his storeroom new treasures as well as old" (Matthew 13:52). He is responsible not only to master the contents of both Old and New Testaments for his own benefit but he must become proficient in handling and using them for the instruction of others. To study how to do this properly, which is the purpose of this little book, is therefore of paramount importance. But before we embark upon this enquiry let us give our attention to some foundational matters.

The importance of this investigation

1. The whole Bible is God's Word. Therefore we must do more than take an interest in what it says. We must be willing to spend a good deal of effort and hard work in understanding a volume which is God's message to the human race. ". . . when you received the word of God, which you heard from us, you accepted it not as the word of men, but as it actually is, the word of God" (I Thessalonians 2:13).

2. The Bible is a divine message to us. It is like a letter sent to us from heaven. It is up to us therefore, to pay the closest attention to what God is saying. We surely should want to understand the meaning of every word.

3. Those who are God's heralds are under obligation not only to understand the message for themselves, but to be

proficient in making it plain to others. If it were necessary at any time to read and explain a letter to some illiterate or blind person how careful we should be to ascertain exactly what the writer of the letter intended to convey, and then to interpret it correctly to our hearer. Even so with the transmission and interpretation of the divine message, we dare not add anything or subtract anything. We must not exaggerate God's truth nor attempt to dress it up in any way to make it more palatable or attractive.

Some difficulties attending this investigation

1. It would be foolish to expect that poor mortals like ourselves would be able to understand God's word all at once. "As the heavens are higher than the earth, so are . . . my thoughts than your thoughts" (Isaiah 55:9). There are many different kinds of teaching in the Bible. When we read it superficially some parts will appear to contradict other parts.
2. Even amongst those of us who fully accept the scriptures as God's authoritative message and recognise them as the final court of appeal in all religious controversies, differences of interpretation arise because we have not as yet reached "unity in the faith . . . and become mature" (Ephesians 4:13). Moreover, there are always sects who, claiming to use the Bible as their authority, teach and spread false doctrine. We can only escape such mistakes if we understand and apply correct rules of interpretation whenever we attempt to teach and expound the scriptures.
3. The sixty-six books which make up the divine library were written in a number of different places and at various times stretching over a period of 1,600 years, beginning 1,500 B.C. and ending 100 A.D. It is probable that some difficulties arising from our study will be cleared up if we know a little about the time, place, authorship and general background of the particular part of the Bible

we are dealing with. The greater part of the Old Testament was written in Hebrew, some few passages in Aramaic; the New Testament was written in Greek. Some problems are likely to arise involving the grammar and idiom of these languages.

Some qualities necessary to this investigation

To study and understand scripture properly and to be able to teach others demands:

    Prayerful diligence
    Hard work that is not discouraged by difficulties
    Perseverance

Bible study without prayer is useless. Preaching truth that we have stored up in our heads but not experienced in heart and life is also useless. The good Christian worker is the one who patiently perseveres in the study of the scriptures throughout the whole term of his ministry and life. "He who prays well will study well" someone has said. The man who would derive real benefit from the study of the scripture must be:

    a spiritual man, i.e. a born again man (John 3:3 and I Corinthians 2:14)
    a humble man (Psalm 25:9)
    an obedient man (John 7:17)
    a prayerful man (Psalm 119:18; James 1:5)

Basic tools and helps to the study of the Bible

A study Bible

Apart from smaller and perhaps more attractively bound Bibles which you will carry around with you and take to the meetings of your church, invest in a study Bible with marginal references, some margin space for notes, and clear and easy to be read print; and make sure it is well bound. You would not normally take this Bible around with you and you would expect it to last a long time — so it is worthwhile to get the best you can but remember, in this case, "best" means the most durable and not the most beautiful.

A reliable modern version

Assuming, though this may not always be the case, that your wide margin reference study Bible is the King James or "Authorised" version of 1611, then you will need at least one modern translation.

The Revised Version (1881/1885), the Revised Standard Version and the New American Standard Bible all have much to commend them as study Bibles but all have, at the same time, disadvantages of one sort or another. Now that the New International Version has become available, and is daily gaining ever wider acceptance, this may be the wisest choice for those who do not want to clutter up their bookshelves with all the modern translations.

Since this book was first published an up-dated edition of the Authorised Version has also become available and this may well be what many readers of this book will prefer.

Concordance and Bible Dictionary

The Concordance will help you track down passages of the Bible that you cannot at once lay your hands on and will also help with the study of Bible words.

The Bible Dictionary will supply you with an immense amount of background material. The IVF "New Bible Dictionary"[1] is probably the best one volume dictionary available while Young's Analytical[2] and Strong's Exhaustive[3] are the standard larger English concordances. If these latter prove too expensive then a good Cruden[4] or even the kind of concordance material you will find at the back of some study Bibles may prove sufficient and certainly better than no concordance at all.

Commentaries

Time in which to use them, space in which to keep them

and money with which to buy them may all prove limiting factors for the ordinary Bible student. A few good books well used are much to be preferred to a whole library of volumes that you cannot make proper use of. Do consult your minister or some other experienced person before spending money on commentaries. Do not be discouraged if, for any reason, you are not able to acquire any or all of the helps listed in this paragraph. Even if you have nothing more than one ordinary Bible and a note book, those diligently used with much prayer will, under the blessing of God, make you a well instructed and a very useful Christian.

Four basic rules that must be observed in interpreting Scripture

1. Interpret with a proper regard for grammatical usage and the plain meaning of words.
2. Interpret with due regard to the immediate context.
3. Interpret with due regard to the character and purpose of the book of the Bible in which your text is found.
4. Interpret with due regard to the teaching of the whole Bible. Scripture is its own interpreter; compare Scripture with Scripture.

2.
Pay attention to grammar

The first of our four basic rules is: *interpret Scripture with a proper regard for grammatical usage and the plain meaning of words.*

Chapter and verse divisions

Although for purposes of reference and for congregational use chapter and verse divisions are invaluable, indeed inevitable, we should remember that the arrangements with which we are so familiar are not very ancient, having been worked out for the Old Testament by Mordecai Nathan in 1445 and for the New Testament by Robert Stephens in 1551. There are a number of places where we may be forgiven for thinking that Stephens and his fellows "nodded"; but whether they did or not, it is as well sometimes to read the scriptures in the way in which their first readers would have done. Let us ignore the chapters and verses and read at a sitting a whole book or considerable sections of a book.

A few examples of unfortunate chapter divisions in our Bibles:

1. The narrative of II Kings 7 seems to begin in II Kings 6:24.

2. The prophetic message contained in Isaiah 53 may be considered to begin with chapter 52:13.

3. It is helpful sometimes to begin the reading of Joshua 6 from chapter 5:13 and to regard 6:1 as being a parenthesis.

Although not suggesting for a moment that parenthetical passages (whether so marked in our Bibles or not) are unimportant or inferior in respect of inspiration, it is useful sometimes for the student to omit such passages for the sake of perceiving clearly the flow of the narrative or the thrust of the message.

4. Only a very unimaginative or insensitive person would read in public Exodus 5 and stop where the chapter stops with the words " ... and you have not rescued your people at all"! Lift your own heart and the hearts of your hearers by running on into the 6th chapter and reading: "Now you will see what I will do to Pharaoh".

5. II Corinthians 7:1 looks like the last verse of the preceding chapter.

6. Similarly Colossians 4:1 looks as though it should have been included in the preceding chapter and labelled 3:26.

7. There are textual problems surrounding the passage beginning John 7:53 and ending John 8:11, but, in any case, it seems odd to find "Then each went to his home" at the end of chapter 7 and "But Jesus went to the Mount of Olives" at the beginning of chapter 8. Versions which arrange the text in paragraphs usually attach 7:53 to 8:1 (no doubt because of the textual problem alluded to above) as for example the 1881 R.V. The more logical arrangement would be to attach 8:1 to 7:53.

8. Isaiah 4:1 would seem to be more appropriately printed as the final verse of chapter 3:27.

Punctuation

For many centuries Hebrew writing was unpunctuated as well as being without vowels. A system of vowel signs was invented during the 7th century A.D.[1] and from that time marks of punctuation were also introduced.

It is probable that Greek was also normally written without punctuation. Certainly the surviving uncial manuscripts do not use punctuation. Uncial manuscripts were

written in Greek capital letters. Two of the most important of these are in the British Museum, but if you cannot
get to the Museum there is an excellent reproduction of a
page from the Sinai Uncial manuscript in 'Nothing But
the Truth".[2] There you will also find a reproduction of a
truly beautiful page of Greek which makes, in the early
16th century, normal use of full stops, commas and other
punctuation.[3]

A few examples of the differences made by punctuation:
1. Most modern translations have decided against the
Authorised Version in respect of the punctuation of Psalm
121:1. The New International Version reads:
>   "I lift up my eyes to the hills —
>   where does my help come from?"

2. John 12:27. Did Jesus say: "Save me from this hour",
or: "Shall I say, 'Save me from this hour?'". The King
James Version and the 1881 Revised Version decide in
favour of the former though the Revised Version makes
room for the latter in the margin. Amongst modern
versions, the New American Standard Bible, the Revised
Standard Version and the New International Version
decide in favour of the latter view.

3. Isaiah 45:11. This appears to be an invitation issued by
God Himself encouraging His people to ask for information concerning the future and to command Him in
reference to His sons. But if a question mark or a note
of exclamation is used instead of a full stop then what
appears to be an invitation to importunate prayer could
be changed into a sharp protest against the arrogance of
people who presumed to issue instructions to Almighty
God. ". . . do you question me about my children, or give
me orders about the work of my hands?" (New International Version). And this appears to harmonise with the
two verses immediately preceding. However, the English
Revised Version (1881) and the New American Standard
Bible do not support this change in punctuation.

4. John 7:37, 38. The margin of the Revised Standard

Version suggests a change in the punctuation of this passage so that it reads: "If any one thirst let him come unto Me, and let him who believes in Me drink. As the scripture has said . . .". This is an attractive way out of difficulties raised by attributing to the Old Testament the saying "out of his (the believer's) inmost being shall flow rivers . . ." But William Hendriksen in his excellent commentary on John hotly contests the re-punctuation, and students would be well advised to read his important discussion of the matter.[4] However, it should be noted that not only does the New English Bible incorporate this re-punctuation in its text but the New International Version dignifies it with a more than ordinarily prominent marginal notice.

Before leaving the important matter of punctuation it is necessary to warn that we are not at liberty to "monkey around" with full stops, commas and question marks to suit our prejudices. This has been done notoriously by the Jehovah's Witnesses in their interpretation of Luke 23:43 where, by the deft transference of a mere comma, they make "Truly I say to you, today you shall be with Me in Paradise" read "Truly I say unto you today, you shall be with Me in Paradise".

It is not only heretical cults that are guilty of this sort of "fiddling". So highly esteemed a Bible teacher as the late G. Campbell Morgan argues strenuously in his commentary on John for the transference of a full stop from the end of 9:3 to the middle of the verse so that for him the passage read: "It was neither that this man sinned or his parents. But in order that the works of God might be displayed in Him, we must work the works of Him who sent me while it is day . . ."[5] The idea that this man might have been born blind to provide a platform for the display of God's glory seemed so monstrous to Campbell Morgan that he resorted to this means of extricating himself. I do not know of any modern version that follows

Morgan at this point and the New English Bible is peculiarly emphatic in support of the view he disliked so much, reading: "It is not that this man or his parents sinned, Jesus answered; he was born blind that God's power might be displayed in curing him."

The mood and tense of verbs

Attention to certain verb forms and to the peculiar force conveyed by the tenses of the Greek language will often help us in matters of interpretation. A number of examples are, therefore, set out below:

1. *John 5:39, 40* "Search the Scriptures . . ." The form of the Greek verb used can be either imperative mood, as in the King James Version, or indicative mood, as in most modern versions. There is, in fact, no way in which we can decide whether this particular verb form is a command (imperative) or a statement of fact (indicative mood) except by consulting the immediate context and circumstances.

It was not necessary to urge the Jews to search the scriptures. They were past masters in the art and most of them had committed to memory large parts of the Old Testament scriptures. Their mistake was the failure to recognise in Jesus, the Messiah of whom those scriptures everywhere spoke. So the New International Version rightly translates: "You diligently study the Scriptures because you think that by them you possess eternal life. These are the Scriptures that testify about me, yet you refuse to come to me to have life". But it is right to point out that both the New American Standard Bible and the New International Version concede in their margins the possibility of an imperative translation.

2. *Romans 5:1* Should we read "We have peace with God" (indicative mood) or "Let us have peace with God" (optative mood)? The King James Version gives us the

former and is followed by a number of modern versions. The 1881 Revised Version and the New English Bible give us the latter. From the Revised Version onwards all versions whatever reading they adopt are careful to warn us in their margins of the alternative. The doubt arises because some ancient manuscripts have *"echomen"* (a short 'o' in the middle) which is indicative and must be translated "we have" and other manuscripts have *"echō-men"* (with the long 'o' or omega in the middle) which is optative and must be translated "Let us have". Bp. Handley Moule in his excellent commentary on Romans has a very interesting discussion of this variant reading.[6] He concedes that the optative reading has far better manuscript authority but concludes that this is one case where the context must be allowed to decide. Bruce Metzger in his Textual commentary on the Greek New Testament informs us that the United Bible Societies Committee came to the same conclusion.[7]

3. *I John 3:9* Here it is the tense of the verb which is important. In this verse the tense used implies a continuous or habitual sinning and it is this that the regenerate man is said to be incapable of. It would be untrue and contrary to experience and contrary to other statements of this book (see 1:7, 8; 5:16, 17) to assert that the child of God can never sin at all. But on the basis of this and similar passages we may very well doubt the spiritual experience of anyone who deliberately persists in a course of habitual sin.

4. *I John 1:7* "the blood of Jesus, his Son, purifies us from every sin". Here again the tense of the verb indicates present time and continuous action. So it is probably right to amplify "keeps on cleansing us from all sin". The New English Bible tries to do this by translating: "we are being cleansed from every sin". However, we must beware lest we pervert this blessed assurance of present cleansing into an excuse for careless living.

Idiomatic language

Every language has expressions which seem to defy normal grammatical rules. An idiom is an expression characteristic of a particular language which cannot be explained by the ordinary rules of logic or grammar. An example of idiom in the English language is the bewildering variety in the use of the preposition "up". There appears, to the foreigner at any rate, to be no particular rhyme or reason in the use of this short word in such phrases as: "look up"; "move up"; "eat up"; "dry up"; "shut up" and "wash-up".

Translators, who try to reduce paraphrasing to a minimum (it can never be eliminated entirely), inevitably reproduce some of these idiomatic expressions in their translations. Hebraisms are, therefore, found in the Greek of the New Testament and also in many English versions.

1. Those who possess a certain quality are said to be "sons" or "children" of that quality:—

I Samuel 2:12 "sons of Belial" (King James Version) becomes "wicked men" (New International Version). Belial was the name of a Palestinian demon and meant "wicked" or "worthless".

Luke 10:6 "son of peace" (King James Version) becomes "man of peace" (New International Version).

Ephesians 2:3 "children of wrath"
          5:6 "sons of disobedience"
          5:8 "children of light"

2. The words "love" and "hate" are used in accordance with Semitic idiom. To love one and hate another may not mean more than to prefer one before the other:—

Luke 14:26 "If anyone comes to Me and does not hate his father and mother . . ." Clearly, in this place, the Semitic idiom must be borne in mind when interpreting, otherwise we make one scripture contradict another.

Romans 9:13 "Jacob I loved, but Esau I hated". Whether the application of the interpretative principle here really does reduce the sense of difficulty which we all must feel with this verse is a matter of opinion. However, it could mean: "To Esau I have granted worldly goods, but to Jacob eternal good". But whatever the difficulties, this passage must teach unconditional election; to make it mean anything less would be unfair to the context.

3. Some absolute statements must be interpreted relatively:—

Genesis 45:8 "It was not you . . . but God . . ." There is, of course, no doubt that Joseph's brothers were responsible for the crime of selling their younger brother into Egypt. "It was not you" means "it was not only (merely, or, chiefly) you, who with evil intention, sold me into Egypt BUT it was, far more importantly, GOD who, with good intent and in His over-arching providence, permitted you to do so and who may, therefore, be said to have sent me." Joseph saw, preferred to see, the good hand of God rather than the jealous and evil hand of his brothers.

Exodus 16:8 "Who are we? You are not grumbling against us, but against the Lord". This appears to contradict 16:2. The meaning plainly must be: "Your murmurings are not only (not chiefly) against us (we are only servants) but (far more seriously) against the Lord (whose servants and representatives we are)".

Mark 9:37 "Whoever welcomes me does not welcome me (not only or chiefly me) but (also, more importantly) the one who sent me". To receive Jesus is to receive Him who sent Him. To receive little children (Mark 9:36, 37) and those who are weak in faith (Romans 14:1) is to receive Jesus.

I Thessalonians 4:8 "Therefore he who rejects this instruction does not reject man (not only, or chiefly, man) but God."

4. In some places the names of parents are used for their descendants. For example, the names "Jacob" and

"Israel" are used not only of Isaac's younger son but of all his descendants (Psalm 14:7; 46:7). The new and honourable name conferred by God upon His people has today become the name of the country in which the Jewish nation lives and of the spiritual children of Abraham (Romans 14:6; Galatians 6:16).

5. Grand-children are sometimes called sons/children:—

Genesis 46:22 "These are the sons of Rachel, who were born to Jacob — 14 persons in all". But Rachel was the mother of only two sons — Joseph and Benjamin! However, Joseph had two sons and Benjamin ten, and all of them are, in this passage, credited to Rachel.

II Samuel 19:24 "And Mephibosheth the son of Saul". He was, in fact, the grand-son of Saul, the son of Saul's son Jonathan (see II Samuel 4:4 and chapter 9).

6. In some places a grand-father is called father:—

Daniel 5:18 Addressing Belshazzar Daniel says: "O king . . . Nebuchadnezzar your father . . ." But Nebuchadnezzar was not Belshazzar's father; he was his grand-father. Nabonidus, who married Nebuchadnezzar's daughter, became king and reigned from B.C. 556—538. As he was not really interested in his imperial responsibilities he associated his own son Belshazzar with himself as co-ruler. It is for this reason that in Daniel 5:16 Belshazzar was able to offer to Daniel only the third place in the kingdom. His father held the first place and he, the second, so that he could not promise to Daniel any place more exalted than the third.

7. Some numbers are probably intended to have a symbolic and not a literal meaning. The number 10 in such passages as Genesis 24:55; 31:7 and Daniel 1:20 probably means "few", "many" or "much" depending on the context.

The numbers 7 and 70 are sometimes used to indicate completeness as in Psalm 119:164; Proverbs 26:16, 25; Matthew 18:21, 22. The number 1,000 (Revelation 20:4, 5) may similarly be used to indicate a long time of indefinite length.

Proper names

Many kings had the same name
In a country which has had eight Henrys, eight Edwards and six Georges we should hardly be surprised at this.

a. *Pharaoh.* From the time of Abraham until the time of Daniel all Egyptian kings were called by the title Pharaoh though occasionally in Scripture the king's personal name (e.g. Shishak I Kings 14:25) is used rather than the imperial title (cf. II Kings 23:29 with II Chronicles 35:20).

b. *Ptolemy.* From the time of Alexander the Great and for about three centuries the rulers of Egypt were known by the new title of Ptolemy after the name of the general of Alexander's who founded the dynasty. Although this name does not appear in the Bible it does illustrate what was a common practice in the Ancient Near East.

c. *Abimelech* was the dynastic or family name of the kings of Philistia (Palestine). Genesis 20:2; 26:1; Psalm 34 title.

d. *Benhadad* was the name borne by many, though not all, of the Syrian kings. I Kings 20:1; II Kings 8:7 and 13:24.

e. *Herod.* Four kings mentioned in the New Testament bear this name. As many readers of the New Testament become confused by the Herods a simple family tree of the Herod family is set out below:—

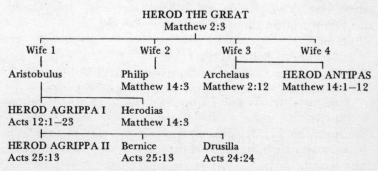

HEROD THE GREAT
Matthew 2:3

Wife 1	Wife 2	Wife 3	Wife 4
Aristobulus	Philip Matthew 14:3	Archelaus Matthew 2:12	HEROD ANTIPAS Matthew 14:1—12
HEROD AGRIPPA I Acts 12:1—23	Herodias Matthew 14:3		
HEROD AGRIPPA II Acts 25:13	Bernice Acts 25:13	Drusilla Acts 24:24	

f. *Caesar.* A family name of the great Julius became a kingly and imperial title adopted not only by Roman emperors but later by the Germans (KAISER) and by the Russians (CZAR). The Caesars referred to in the gospels are Augustus (Luke 2:1) and elsewhere Tiberius; and in the Acts, Claudius (11:28; 17:7; 18:2) and elsewhere Nero, although this personal name is never used in the New Testament.

Some people had two names

a. The father-in-law of Moses seems sometimes to have been known as Jethro (Exodus 3:1) and sometimes as Hobab (Judges 4:11).

b. Levi (Mark 2:14) and Matthew (Matthew 9:9; 10:3) were the same person — a tax-gatherer, and then one of the twelve apostles, and author of the first gospel.

c. Thomas called Didymus (John 11:16; 20:24; 21:2). The name Didymus means "Twin" (see John 11:16 Revised Standard Version). The name Didymus appears only in John's gospel.

d. Saul (from Acts 7:58 to 13:9).
   Paul (from Acts 13:9 to end of book).

e. Silas (Acts 18:5) is also Silvanus (II Corinthians 1:19).

Two people with the same name

Again it may be remarked that in a country where we have so many Bakers, Smiths, Browns and Joneses and where we have so many Johns, Roberts, and Davids this complication should hardly surprise us.

a. James
   i. Brother of John (Mark 1:19)
       One of the 12 apostles (Matthew 10:2)
       Beheaded by Herod Agrippa I (Acts 12:2)
   ii. Brother of the Lord Jesus (Matthew 13:55; Galatians 1:19)
        Leading pastor/elder of Jerusalem church (Acts 15:13; Galatians 2:12)
        Author of the epistle (James 1:1)

b. Philip
   i. One of the 12 (Matthew 10:3; John 6:5; 12:21; 14:8)
   ii. One of the 7 (Acts 6:5; 21:8)
     The evangelist (Acts 8:5, 26; 21:8)

Different places with the same name
We have at least two Bradfords, two Stratfords and two Bromleys in England.
a. Caesarea can be either:—
   i. Caesarea Philippi (Matthew 16:13), lies to the north of Sea of Galilee, east of River Jordan and south of Mount Hermon, or
   ii. A sea-port on the Mediterranean coast (Acts 10:1; 12:19; 23:23), located in the province of Samaria.
b. Antioch can be either:—
   i. Syrian Antioch (Acts 11:20, 26; 13:1), lies north of Damascus and of Tyre and Sidon, and east of Cyprus, or
   ii. Pisidian Antioch (Acts 13:14, II Timothy 3:11), to the north-west of Syrian Antioch.

Places with two or more names
a. Egypt is called:—
   i. Ham (Psalm 78:51; 105:23)
   ii. Rahab (Psalm 87:4; 89:10; Isaiah 51:9)
   iii. Mizraim (Genesis 10:6, 13; 50:11; I Chronicles 1:8, 11)
b. Jerusalem is called:—
   i. Zion (Psalm 137:1 and many other places)
   ii. Ariel "the city where David encamped" (Isaiah 29:1)
c. Sinai is also called Horeb (Psalm 106:19)
d. Sea of Galilee is also called:—
   i. Tiberias (John 21:1 and 6:1)
   ii. Sea of Chinnereth (Numbers 34:11)
e. Dead Sea — This name does not occur in the Bible. It is called "the sea of the plain" (II Kings 14:25); "the eastern sea" (Ezekiel 47:18; Zechariah 14:8) and "the salt sea" (Genesis 14:3; Numbers 34:3, 12)

f. The Mediterranean — This name also does not occur in the Bible. Instead it is called "sea of the Philistines" (Exodus 23:31); "the uttermost sea" (Deuteronomy 11:24; 34:2; Joel 2:20) and "the great sea" (Numbers 34:6, 7)

The first basic rule of interpretation requires us to pay attention to the plain meaning of words and to ordinary grammatical usage.

3.
Pay attention to context

The second basic principle to be borne in mind when seeking to interpret scripture is: *interpret with due regard to the immediate context.*

Failure to observe this rule has resulted in the spread of heretical doctrine and where consequences have not been as serious as this a good many ludicrous and absurd interpretations have helped to bring the scriptures and the pulpit into disrepute.

Many years ago I remember reading in a book devoted to the peculiar views of the British Israel cult a remarkable interpretation of the blessing pronounced by Moses upon Joseph (Deuteronomy 33:16) where "the good will of him that dwelt in the bush" (AV) was made to mean the good will of those who live in the South African bush rather than the good will of the Angel of the Lord who appeared to Moses in the burning bush! And then quite recently when reading a book about Jehovah's Witnesses I was startled to meet a novel way of using Joel 2:3. Manifestly, the passage describes the devastations of a cloud of locusts who finding a garden of Eden before them leave a desolate wilderness behind them. The book I was reading repeatedly spoke of the desolating experiences of persecutions that were behind the Witnesses and of the golden age garden of Eden that is before them!

However, if the cults are the worst and most blatant offenders they are most certainly not the only offenders. I came across a laughable example a few years ago in India. The offender was a very able and greatly used pastor/evangelist and he had, moreover, three years of Bible school behind him. I was therefore all the more disconcerted when I observed his method. He was speaking

to a group of pastors who had been gathered together
for a few days of quiet retreat. In Anglo-Indian vocabu-
lary whenever you are away from home or from your
headquarters you are on "camp". So our preacher friend
thought of us as being on camp and then proceeded to
look up the word "camp" in a concordance. He selected
ten uses of the word stretching from Exodus to Revelation
which appeared to him to suit his purpose and then
described to us what he thought should characterise our
time spent together in conference. (This, by the way, is a
dubious way of using a concordance). On the basis of
Exodus 32:17, 18 he told us that our camp should be
characterised by singing, ignoring the context which
makes it plain that the singing on that occasion was
deplorable and lascivious. In other words, precisely the
kind of song one would least expect to hear in a gather-
ing of ministers of the gospel!

In order to interpret with due regard for the immediate
context we must take notice of seven matters.

1. *A word may have more than one meaning and the
context must help us to decide*
a. Faith is one such word. It has four different meanings in the New Testament:—
   i. In some contexts it means "the gospel" (Galatians
       1:23, I Timothy 3:9; 4:1).
   ii. In Romans 14:23 the word "faith" appears to mean
       "good" or "clear conscience".
   iii. In some contexts, particularly in the Hebrews epistle,
       faith seems to mean a trust in the reliability of the
       divine promises, and is not always clearly to be dis-
       tinguished from "hope".
   iv. In Romans 3:28 and generally throughout the New
       Testament and particularly in the Pauline epistles
       "faith" is a whole-hearted resting in Christ and in
       His atoning work as the ground of pardon and peace.
       This is "saving faith".

b. Flesh is another such word. It has at least three different meanings in the New Testament:—

    i. Its ordinary meaning — a human body and human nature without implying anything as to sinfulness or sinlessness (John 1:14; Romans 1:3 and 9:3).

    ii. The word "flesh" is however more commonly used in the New Testament to mean fallen human nature (Romans 8:5 and Ephesians 2:3).

    iii. The word "flesh" is sometimes used of outward and merely ceremonial religion as distinct from the inward and spiritual (Galatians 3:3; 6:12; Philippians 3:3).

A comparison of the Authorized Version translation of two of these passages with the New International Version will illustrate admirably this particular use of the word "flesh".

    Galatians 3:3 "Are ye so foolish? having begun in the Spirit, are ye now made perfect by the flesh?" becomes in the New International Version:— "Are you so foolish? After beginning with the Spirit, are you now trying to attain your goal by human effort?"

    Galatians 6:12 "As many as desire to make a fair show in the flesh" . . . becomes in the New International Version:— "Those who want to make a good impression outwardly".

c. Salvation is yet another word which has several different meanings:—

    i. It is occasionally used to denote physical or national deliverance:—

    Exodus 14:13; Judges 2:16; 3:9, 15 (R.V.)

    Acts 7:25 (RV mg/Gk). Acts 27:20 "all hope of our being saved".

    These various experiences of deliverance may be regarded as shadows and types of spiritual salvation.

    ii. It is sometimes used of the healing of the sick. James 5:15 (AV)

    iii. It is, however, mostly used of those spiritual

blessings which come to us through faith in Christ —
sometimes referring to immediate and present
deliverance as in Ephesians 2:8 and Luke 1:77
and sometimes referring to the consummation for
which we still wait as in Romans 13:11 and I Peter
1:5.

2. *The context may limit the application of a word or
statement*

Let us consider a few examples:—

a. "Judge me . . . according to my righteousness" (Psalm
7:8; 18:20).

David is not claiming to be righteous in the absolute
sense; he is, however, in Psalm 7, conscious of being
innocent in respect of the malicious accusations brought
against him by Cush. He therefore, in this place as in many
others, confidently asks God to vindicate him. Job also, in
the same sense, asserts his righteousness in many places.

b. "Neither this man, nor his parents sinned" (John 9:3).

This, of course, does not mean that this blind man or
his parents were sinlessly perfect. All it means is that
neither the man himself nor his parents had committed
any special sin which might be regarded as the immediate
cause of his blindness.

c. "The prayer of faith shall save the sick" James 5:15
(AV).

The context indicates that "save" means "heal". The
passage allows no support to the Romish practice of
extreme unction and it is doubtful whether it allows any
support to the practice of public healing meetings.

d. "It is good for a man not to touch a woman" I Corinthians 7:1 (AV).

In view of the context it cannot mean that it is good
for a man not to marry (see also Hebrews 13:4). It could
however be argued from the context that Paul is recom-
mending that in the dangerous circumstances of the times
it might be wise to refrain from marriage (see 7:26).

In a grossly immoral situation this verse may mean that it is good (contrary to a common opinion both then and now) for an unmarried man not to touch a woman. After marriage, it is plainly not good for a man to refrain from touching his wife (1 Corinthians 7:3—5) except in special circumstances.

3. *The use of irony — the context requires us to understand the words in the very opposite of their natural sense*
For example:
a. When Baalam, who had already made up his own mind, repeatedly asked God whether he might go or not, in response to Balak's invitation, the Lord appears to give him permission saying: "Rise up and go" (Numbers 22:20 AV). But the context makes it abundantly plain that his going was not God's will (see 22:22). God's apparent permission: "Rise up and go" really means: "If, after all I have told you, your heart is set on violating my command, do it at your own risk".
b. I Kings 22:15 "Go, and prosper . . . " (AV). These words of Micaiah were recognised as ironic mockery by King Ahab. Either the tone of voice in which the words were spoken or the look on Micaiah's face must have made this obvious to the wicked but perceptive monarch. Micaiah's real views are made plain in 22:17.
c. I Kings 18:27 ". . . Elijah began to taunt them. 'Shout louder! . . . Surely he is a god! . . .' "
Plainly the statement "Surely he is a god" is not to be regarded as a serious theological statement. It is merely part of the little piece of mockery that Elijah indulged in with the idea of exposing Baal worship to the ridicule of the spectators — the crowds of people who were wavering between two opinions (I Kings 18:21).
d. "Already you have all you want! Already you have become rich" (I Corinthians 4:8).
Paul is probably here quoting the arrogant and complacent claims made for themselves by the Corinthian Christians (cf. Revelation 3:17).

4. *Some traditional interpretations that should be looked at again in the light of this rule*

a. "Choose for yourselves this day whom you will serve . . ." (Joshua 24:15).

This passage is frequently used in evangelistic gatherings as a warrant for urging people to choose the Lord Jesus Christ. But Joshua does not appear to be saying anything like this; but rather: "You do not appear to want to serve the Lord; very well, then, choose whom you will serve. And this is the wretched choice that lies before you; either the gods that your ancestors served in Mesopotamia, or the gods of this land in which you are now settled." If we turn our backs upon God then we are left with a beggarly choice between one idol and another.

The writer does not maintain that it is absolutely wrong to use this passage in an evangelistic sense but he does insist that it must be wrong completely to ignore the context as is so commonly done.

b. "Here am I; send me. And He said, Go and tell this people . . ." (Isaiah 6:8, 9).

How many missionary challenges have been based upon this passage and upon these words! And how many of God's servants trace their call to some occasion when God appeared to be saying to them: "Whom shall I send, and who will go for us?" But how few really face the problems that are raised by the following verses in which we discover that what Isaiah was to "tell this people", far from being good news appears to have been very bad news, (See Matthew 13:10—17 and Acts 28:25—28).

c. "Thy people shall be willing in the day of thy power" Psalm 110:3 (AV).

There can be no doubt whatever that sinners become willing to seek the Lord and to ask forgiveness for their sins only when God graciously puts forth His power, by the Holy Spirit, and makes them willing. There are many passages of scripture which can be adduced to support this doctrine. But can Psalm 110:3 rightly be used in this way?

The whole context speaks of a summons to holy warfare. "The day of Thy power" probably means "The day of calling up soldiers for an army". A "power" was a Shakespearean expression for an army (see Henry IV Part 1 Sc 1 line 22 "Forthwith a power of English shall we levy"). The atmosphere of Psalm 110 is very much like what we find in Judges 5:2 and 9 "the people willingly offered themselves". (See Psalm 110:3 in N.I.V.).

5. *Parenthetical passages*

a. Sometimes the main flow of a narrative is interrupted by a brief digression intended to convey some piece of information:—

i. Joshua 6:1 appears to be such a digression, introduced to inform us of the state of siege that Jericho was in. Most Bibles do not indicate by brackets that this is a parenthesis and that fact added to the chapter division helps to obscure the link between 5:15 and 6:2. The writer distinctly remembers the impression made upon him when he first heard the passages 5:13 to 6:2 read, omitting 6:1.

ii. Daniel 2:4. The words "in Aramaic" are probably a brief parenthetical comment intended to indicate not that the Chaldeans spoke in that language (though that was undoubtedly the case) but that the narrative from that point on to the end of chapter seven is written in the Aramaic (or Syriack) language instead of in Hebrew.

iii. In John chapter 1 there are three such brief comments all of them being interpretations into Greek of Hebrew names or titles, i.e. Rabbi, Messiah and Cephas. In the King James Version only the first of these is placed within brackets; all should be treated alike.

b. There are some sacred writers, notably Paul, who appear to indulge in the practice of making quite long digressions. This habit provides us with an illustration of

the way in which Holy Spirit inspiration need not necessarily over-ride the writer's temperament or style of
writing. Paul's was a volatile and passionate temperament
capable of going off at a word; of breaking away from the
main thread of an argument and running on, sometimes
for a few verses and sometimes for several chapters,
before coming back once again to the point where he had
begun to digress. We are not for a moment suggesting that
the parenthetical material is unimportant or uninspired;
on the contrary, some of Paul's parentheses contain
material of utmost theological and ethical significance.

i. An interesting example of "going off at a word" is
to be found in I Thessalonians 2:14—16 where the
mention of "Jews" at the end of verse 14 evidently
lights a flame of mingled astonishment and resent-
ment which leads him in the next two verses to
describe the stiff-necked attitude of his own people
and the doom which they were bringing upon themselves. What he deals with briefly here he writes
about more fully in II Corinthians 3 and, at greater
length still, in the famous Romans 9—11 passage.

ii. Most commentators seem to think that we have one
or more such digressions in Ephesians 3 but there is
not total agreement as to where the digressions begin
and end.
3:1 "For this reason I Paul . . ." seems to be picked
up again in verse 14 "For this reason I bow . . ." in
which case the parenthesis would be 3:2 to 3:13. On
the other hand the phrase in 3:1 "the prisoner
of . . ." seems to be picked up again in 4:1 "As a
prisoner of the Lord then" in which case the whole
of the third chapter, or 3:2—3:21 might be regarded
as digression. For some reason, Scofield Bible
suggests that verses 13—21 are parenthetical.

iii. Perhaps the longest digression, if it may justly be
called that, occurs in the passage II Corinthians 2:14
to 7:5. The mention of Titus in 2:13 is picked up

again in 7:6. The unspeakable relief and joy which came to an overwrought spirit by the arrival of Titus led Paul to forget to say any more just then about his young friend and to run off into a paean of praise and then into more than four chapters of exalted writing which is not always easy to follow.

iv. Romans 5 provides us with an interesting example. In verse 12 we have an incomplete sentence; this is indicated in Revised Version (1881) and in the New American Standard Bible by a dash. The main drift of the argument is resumed in verse 18 so that verses 13—17 are parenthetical and this is indicated in King James Version (1611) by the use of brackets. There is an interesting discussion of this passage and of the relationship of so called "literary style" to scripture in Dr Martyn Lloyd Jones's volume on this chapter entitled "Assurance".[1] In the same volume the distinguished preacher/commentator describes chapters 6 and 7 of Romans as parenthetical "an interruption of the main argument, to deal with two major difficulties and objections".[2]

6. *Covert dialogue*

There are a number of passages in the Bible where a dialogue is apparently being carried on between the writer of the book and some other person or persons:—

a. We find such a dialogue clearly set out in the early part of the brief prophecy of Habakkuk with the prophet protesting to God in 1:1—4 and again in 1:12—2:1 and with God Himself condescending to justify His ways to His puzzled servant in 1:5—11 and 2:2—4.

b. Running throughout the Romans Epistle there are evidences of the kind of debate that must often have taken place between the disputatious Jewish scribes and the apostle Paul. They are the very questions Paul himself would have asked in his old persecuting days.

Such as:— 3:1 "What advantage then is there in being a

Jew? or what value is there in circumcision?" Paul gives a brief answer in the next verse and a rather longer answer in 9:4, 5. (See also 3:3, 4; 3:5, 6; 3:8; 6:1, 2; 6:15; 7:7; 9:6; 9:14.)

However, in fairness, it must be stated that some commentators believe that to state the matter in this way is to overstate it and that we have little more in these passages than a series of rhetorical questions that suggest themselves to the apostle as he is writing and which he introduces to make his writing more vivid and powerful.

7. *Quoting an opponent*

In the Corinthian letters we find a style of writing which creates far more difficulties for us, probably, than anything else so far discussed. We refer to Paul's habit of quoting either from letters that he had received or from derogatory remarks that were in circulation about himself. Where he makes it clear that he is so quoting we have no problem but there are a number of places where he does not make it clear:—

a. "Everything is permissible for me" (I Corinthians 6:12; 10:23).

This is almost certainly something that the Corinthian Christians were saying to themselves to quieten their consciences with respect to certain things they were allowing in their conduct. Paul is not necessarily disagreeing with them but he is adding certain cautionary riders.

b. "Food for the stomach and the stomach for food" (6:13).

This too is a saying that had become almost proverbial amongst the Corinthians. What they meant by it was "the gratification of bodily needs is morally indifferent". This argument was not even valid in the comparatively harmless area of eating and drinking but it became far more dangerous when it was extended and made to apply to the gratification of the body's sexual needs by indulgence in fornication. Paul gives a very vigorous rebuttal to this sophistry.

c. "We know that we all possess knowledge" (I Corinthians 8:1). The New International Version suggests in a footnote: "We all possess knowledge as you say". Paul appears to be saying, "This is what your boasted knowledge does to you. It puffs you up. A little less of your knowledge and a little more love is what you need."

d. "I, Paul, who am 'timid' when face to face with you, but 'bold' when away!" (II Corinthians 10:1). The verses following, and a comparison with 10:10 where the references to his critics' derogatory remarks is explicit, make it virtually certain that here too the apostle is quoting some of the unkind remarks about himself that were circulating amongst the discontented section of the church, as the NIV implies by its use of speech marks.

e. "Yet, crafty fellow that I am, I caught you by trickery" (II Corinthians 12:16). Here again it is virtually certain that Paul is quoting the kind of innuendo which was being put into circulation about him in Corinth by his unscrupulous opponents.

When dealing with problems like these it is tempting to resort to the use of some modern paraphrase which does not hesitate to fill out the enigmatic and baffling shorthand style of the writer. If a paraphrase is used as a commentary and not as a translation then there may be no objection to our consulting it. However, we must remember that paraphrases are taken up with interpretation and their interpretations may be wrong!

So, our second basic principle is this: *we must interpret in a manner consistent with the immediate context.*

4.
The larger context

We have so far examined the actual words of the passage
we are concerned to interpret. We have tried to ascertain
their plain meaning using the normal rules of grammar.
Further, we have paid careful attention to the immediate
context, that is to the verses of scripture immediately
preceding and immediately following, to see if what we
believe, at first glance, to be the plain and obvious meaning
may need modification.

We must now move a step further; we must be prepared
to take seriously the larger context within which our
passage is imbedded. This means we must become familiar
with the whole book or section of a book of which our
passage forms a part. Knowledge of the circumstances in
which an author wrote, of the people to whom he wrote
and of the motive or motives with which he wrote are
likely to throw a flood of light upon the passage with
which we are grappling and will quite often compel us to
modify in some way or another our view of what the
passage means and is intended to teach.

However there are some books of the Bible concerning
which we cannot answer all the questions we might wish
to ask. For example, we cannot be sure who wrote the
Epistle to Hebrews nor can we be sure what group of
Hebrew Christians it was addressed to (whether those in
Palestine or those in Italy). But it is possible to gather
from the epistle itself a pretty accurate picture of the
circumstances in which these Hebrew Christians were
living and of the grievous and tempting stresses to which
they were exposed.

The author and circumstances of some books of the Bible

The Epistles of the Apostle Paul
They are here set out in the possible order of their being written although as will be pointed out below there are differences of opinion with respect to some of the books:—

a. *I & II Thessalonians* — These used to be commonly regarded as the first of all Paul's writings and they are still so regarded by many. They were written from Corinth during the apostle's second Missionary Journey, probably in the year A.D. 50.

Make yourself thoroughly familiar with a map of the various journeys made by the Apostle Paul.

b. *I & II Corinthians* — During Paul's third missionary journey the first letter was written from Ephesus in the year A.D. 56 and the second letter from Philippi, probably at the end of the same year or early in A.D. 57.

c. *Galatians and Romans* — It was commonly thought, and is still thought by many, that these were both written from Corinth during the apostle's third journey and in the year A.D. 57. The Galatian epistle was thought to have been written first and to have been a kind of rough draft around which Paul later built the massive theological treatise which he despatched to Rome. However, both the destination and date of the Galatian epistle have been matters of tangled controversy and according to one view Galatians might be the first of our canonical Pauline epistles instead of the fifth.[1]

d. *The Prison Epistles:— Ephesians, Colossians, Philippians and Philemon* were almost certainly written from Rome during the two year period in which the apostle was under house arrest — A.D. 61—63.

As Romans is commonly regarded as being a more fully developed version of Galatians so Ephesians may be a more fully developed version of the Colossian letter.

Philemon was a wealthy member of the Colossian

church. The letter addressed to him was sent along with the letter to the church by the hand of the runaway slave Onesimus (see Colossians 4:9).

Of the ten letters addressed to churches only two — those to Rome and Colosse — were addressed to churches that Paul had not founded and had never, at the time of writing, visited.

e. *The Pastoral Epistles* — The first letter to Timothy and the letter to Titus were written in a brief interval of freedom that Paul appears to have enjoyed between his "house arrest" imprisonment (Acts 28:30, 31) and the more rigorous imprisonment of which we read in II Timothy. So I Timothy and Titus may have been written in A.D. 65 and II Timothy shortly before the writer's death in A.D. 66 or 67.

The Four Gospels

a. *Matthew* — Even if it is conceded that Mark was the earliest, chronologically, of the four gospels there is an obvious and excellent reason for this gospel standing first in the New Testament volume. The student may discover other examples in the Bible where an over-ruling providence may be discerned in the arranging of the order of the books in disregard of the probable chronological order. Matthew with its opening genealogy and with its concern to illustrate the fulfilment of the Old Testament prophecy provides us with the necessary link between Old and New and is calculated to reassure Hebrew Christians that there is a real continuity and that the New is the fulfilment of the Old. It was written by a Jew primarily for Hebrew Christians. The narrative is built around five long discourses of which the best known is The Sermon on the Mount (chapters 5—7).

b. *Mark* — The five or six New Testament books that were not written by apostles were all written by close companions of apostles. Mark may perhaps be regarded as Peter's account. This book gives a great deal of space

to the wonderful works of Jesus and it is thought to
have been written primarily for Roman Christians.

c. *Luke* — Luke was a close companion of the apostle
Paul and author of the book of Acts as well as of this
third gospel. The book was written in the first place for
an honourable gentleman bearing the Greek name
Theophilus. This gospel includes a large number of
parables; it also pays much more attention to the women
who were connected with the gospel story than do the
other accounts. (But John's gospel is not far behind Luke
in the place it gives to women). These first three gospels
are called "synoptic" gospels because they cover much
the same ground and it is possible to piece them together and so construct, more or less, a running account
or a harmony.

d. *John* — John was the disciple "whom Jesus loved".
He was, possibly, the youngest of the twelve; he was
certainly the longest lived and the only one of them all
who was still alive towards the end of the first century.
There are very considerable and obvious differences
between the "synoptic" gospels and the fourth gospel.
Is it possible that one secondary purpose of the gospel
(the primary purpose is set out unambiguously in 20:31)
was to preserve for the church material that was not
included in the synoptics? There are no parables in this
gospel though there are some allegories. All but two of
the seven miracles reported by John are found only in
the fourth gospel. The ordinary Greek word for miracle
is not used to describe them but another Greek word
meaning sign. (RV and modern translations translate
"signs").

From a very early time it has been the delight of commentators to differentiate one gospel from another by
suggesting symbolic motifs and one very popular plan is
as follows:—

Matthew — presents Christ as KING
         the gospel of the Lion
Mark   — presents Jesus as the perfect SERVANT
         the gospel of the ox
Luke   — presents Jesus as the perfect MAN
         the gospel of the man
John   — presents Jesus as SON OF GOD
         the gospel of the eagle (See Ezekiel 1:10)

The Psalms
The circumstances in which some of the Psalms were
written may be found in the explanatory titles, e.g. Psalms
3, 18, 34, 51, 52, 54, 57, 142. The 90th psalm is called
"A Prayer of Moses the man of God". Psalms 120–134
are called "Songs of Degrees" ("Songs of Ascents" — NIV)
and were songs sung by Jewish pilgrims as they made their
way to Jerusalem for the great national festivals. As they
wended their way through the "mountains round about
Jerusalem" (125:2) they sang "I was glad when they said
unto me . . ." (Psalm 122).

**The purpose behind the writing of some of the books of
the Bible**

A number of Bible books help us by stating quite clearly
what their purpose is:—

The Book of Proverbs
Chapter 1:2, 3, 4 For attaining wisdom and discipline; for
understanding words of insight; for acquiring a disciplined
and prudent life . . . for giving prudence to the simple,
knowledge and discretion to the young.
Chapter 22:19 So that your trust may be in the Lord.
Chapter 22:20, 21 Have not I written to thee . . . that
I might make thee know the certainty of the words of
truth; that thou mightest answer the words of truth to
them that send unto thee (AV).

Gospel according to Luke
Chapter 1:1–4 ". . . it seemed good also to me . . . to write an orderly account for you, most excellent Theophilus, so that you may know the certainty of the things you have been taught".

Gospel according to John
Chapter 20:31 But these are written that you may believe that Jesus is the Christ, the Son of God; and that by believing you may have life in His name.

John's First Epistle
Chapter 5:13 I write these things to you that believe in the name of the Son of God so that you may know that you have eternal life.

Purpose of the Old Testament
Romans 15:4 For every thing that was written in the past was written to teach us, so that through endurance and the encouragement of the Scriptures we might have hope.
I Corinthians 10:11 These things happened to them as examples and were written down as warnings for us . . . .

Purpose of the whole Bible
II Timothy 3:16, 17 All Scripture is . . . useful for teaching, for rebuking, correcting, and training in righteousness, so that the man of God may be thoroughly equipped for every good work.

Apparent contradictions

If we pay attention to the main purpose lying behind the writing of any book or any section of a book in the Bible we may find that apparent contradictions clear up. For example:
1. *Romans 3:28* "A man is justified by faith apart from observing the law."

James 2:24 "A person is justified by what he does and
not by faith alone."

At first glance these two scriptures seem incapable of
reconciliation and hopelessly inconsistent with one
another. At various times in the history of the church
some have felt the difficulty to be so great that they have
been tempted to discard The Epistle of James. Luther
spoke of it as "a right strawy epistle" and even Scofield's
Bible, though quite correct on the main issue, is so mis-
guided as to describe this epistle as "elementary in the
extreme".

The Roman epistle sets out to demonstrate that neither
in the Old Testament dispensation nor at the present time
has any man been justified by the works of the law. Salvation has always been by faith.

James' letter insists that a faith which does not
function, a belief which does not behave, a mental assent
to doctrinal propositions which produces no good works,
will not justify anybody; such a faith is not true faith, is
not saving faith.

It could be argued that Paul and James use the three
vital words "works", "faith" and "justification" in different senses. It amounts to the same thing to say, as Paul
does: "A man is justified by such a faith as must from its
very nature issue in good works" or, as James says:
"A man is justified by such works as can only issue from
a true and living faith". James is refuting either Jewish
bigots who thought that a profession of monotheism
would save them (see 2:19) or mistaken Paulinists who
thought that justification could be divorced from sancti-
fication.

2. *Romans 14:6* "He who regards one day as special,
does so to the Lord."

Galatians 4:9, 10 "How is it that you are turning back
to those weak and miserable principles? Do you wish to
be enslaved by them all over again? You are observing
special days and months and seasons and years!"

The Romans epistle is dealing with the case of certain believers who, having been brought up as Jews, felt bound to continue observance of the Jewish Sabbath and of the Jewish regulations with regard to meats (the avoidance of certain sorts of meat and insistence upon kosher methods of slaughtering). Paul says that we should avoid disputation about doubtful matters and that we should receive into our church fellowship people who may have scruples about such matters. Therefore, in India for example, no one would require that converts from Hinduism should become meat eaters, or, even worse, eaters of beef in order to qualify for church membership.

But the Galatian epistle is conducting a tremendous blitz against Judaizing teachers who were insisting that the seventh day should be observed as a sabbath by all Christians including those from a Gentile background and that the old Jewish dietary laws should be strictly observed (See also Colossians 2:21; I Timothy 4:3). Paul pleads with them not to become again entangled in a yoke of bondage.

So if a believer is a vegetarian for health reasons or even because he or she is not completely emancipated from old custom or scruple we need not and indeed must not harass them or bully them into conforming to our food habits. But if a Jewish convert or a Hindu convert or a Seventh Day Adventist attempts to impose his scruples in these matters upon the rest of the church he must be resisted vigorously. Paul refused to give in for a moment to false teachers "so that the truth of the gospel might remain with" his new converts (Galatians 2:5).

But we must beware of supposing that Romans 14:6 sanctions the continuing observance of heathen festivals, the use of astrological horoscopes to discover auspicious days or the carrying over into our Christian life of old superstitions.

3. *Matthew 19:16, 17* "What good thing must I do to get eternal life? . . . If you want to enter life, obey the

commandments". Also Luke 10:25, 28 "Teacher what must I do to inherit eternal life? . . . Do this and you will live".

Acts 16:30, 31 "What must I do to be saved? Believe in the Lord Jesus and you will be saved."

To some who come asking us religious questions we should preach the demands of God's holy law; to others we should show Christ as the only Saviour and urge them to trust in Him. It is clear that neither the rich young ruler nor the lawyer (Luke 10:25) came with broken hearts and contrite spirits but on the contrary with an exalted sense of their own virtue and of their capacity for doing anything that might be required of them in order to earn eternal life. When confronted by people in this frame of mind it is useless to exhort them to believe in the Lord Jesus Christ; indeed to do so would be very much like casting pearls before swine. It is only the man who is beginning to suspect that he cannot hope to keep the spiritual and inward law of God and that his plight is desperate who will cry out as the Philippian gaoler did. It is the man who is about to sink who cries out: "Lord save me" (Matthew 14:30). The gaoler was ready to be instructed to believe on the Lord Jesus Christ and be saved; he had been prepared by the miraculous work of the Holy Ghost operating upon his heart by means of a midnight earthquake.

There are lessons here for all who undertake personal work. We should preach the gospel in a way suitable to the enquirer, discerning his or her state as best we can. Is it really becoming to urge people who know nothing about the being of God or the attributes of God and nothing about His character and laws to believe on the Lord Jesus Christ? Will such an appeal addressed to such unprepared hearts produce true faith in the lives of those we are dealing with?[2]

Some further examples of interpreting with due regard to the wider context

1. *Luke 15* Whom does the elder brother represent? If we confine our attention to the immediate context the answer is plain enough; the elder brother is clearly a picture of the scribes and pharisees who murmured saying: "This man welcomes sinners and eats with them" (15:2). But if we remember the wider context of the whole gospel and of its sequel, the book of Acts, surely we may extend the application of the parable to the loving reception of the Gentiles and the horrified aloofness of most Jews. Would it be in order to up-date the parable and compare the elder brother to self-righteous members of our churches and congregations who look askance at "way-out" members of our society as, with penitent hearts, they weep their way to the foot of the cross? Our long refrigerated hearts may only be embarrassed by such conversions!

2. *Hebrews 4:3, 5* There are some Bible teachers who insist that the "rest" spoken of in these passages cannot possibly refer to the eternal rest of God's everlasting kingdom. They so argue because the Canaan "rest" towards which the Israelites were journeying included warfare and failure. This "rest" they say is the enjoyment of "the higher life" that is available to the believer here below but which only some attain; it is an experience which we may forfeit and which many do forfeit. Many years ago I read and re-read with much puzzlement a commentary written by a man I knew well in India which attempted with much skill and undoubted piety to apply consistently this method of interpretation. G. H. Lang, a very gifted though not a very orthodox teacher amongst the Christian Brethren advocated similar views and also wrote a commentary on this epistle. According to him there are ordinary Christians and first class Christians called "overcomers" (and a partial rapture in which only the overcomers have a part). When the Lord returns and those which are alive

and remain (I Thessalonians 4:17) are caught up or raptured, those who are not overcomers miss the glories and blessedness of the millennial kingdom. This system if applied consistently leads on to some very disconcerting conclusions. We must make up our mind what is the main purpose of the Hebrew epistle. Its primary purpose, though not necessarily its only purpose, is to warn Hebrew Christians of the danger of apostasy, of the danger of falling away from the Christian religion altogether; any deliberate settling for second class status would be to endanger one's Christian profession and would very probably lead on to apostasy. He warns of those who had a "gospel" preached to them in the wilderness but gained no permanent profit from hearing it (cf also I Corinthians 10:5 "Nevertheless, God was not pleased with most of them; their bodies were scattered over the desert"). Let us make our calling and election sure with fear and trembling "lest while a promise remains of entering His rest, any one of you should seem to have come short of it" 4:1 (AV). You have received the gospel, or so it would seem. Let your present manner of life and adherence to the Christian profession make it plain to yourself and to others that your conversion was genuine conversion. Don't deny the faith; don't crucify to yourself afresh the Son of God and put Him to an open shame.

So in spite of difficulties I am bound to interpret the "rest" as a reference to heavenly rest (though without denying the reality of a present rest and foretaste of heaven). Also, again in spite of difficulties, I have to regard the wilderness wanderings as in many respects typical of the whole of the Christian life of all God's people. Canaan is then in some respects a "type" of the heavenly rest towards which we are journeying. Perhaps here it may not be out of place to point out that we sometimes run ourselves into unnecessary difficulties of interpretation by assuming that, for example, every point of a parable should be susceptible of application or that every detail of Israel's history should be capable of being fitted into a certain typical pattern which we impose upon it.

An example of how the principles may be applied to a particular problem

"Lest having preached to others I myself should be a castaway" I Corinthians 9:27 (AV).

In applying the First Principle which requires us to pay attention to the plain meaning of words we find in our text two words that call for special examination:

1. *"Preached"* — The Greek word so translated means to proclaim as an herald and the preceding context seems to imply a reference to the herald calling competitors into the arena for the Isthmian or other games of the ancient Greek world.

2. *"Castaway"* — The Greek word is *"adokimos"*. *"Dokimos"* means "approved after trial" (Romans 14:8; 16:10; I Corinthians 11:19; II Corinthians 10:18; 13:7; II Timothy 2:15; James 1:12). The "a" is a prefix used in Greek, and in many other languages too, to deny the existence of the thing denoted by the following noun or adjective (e.g. a + theist). This prefix is called *"a"* privative. *"a"* (privative) + *"dokimos"* is usually translated "rejected" or "reprobate" and only here is it translated "castaway" (Jeremiah 6:30; I Corinthians 9:27; Hebrews 6:8; Romans 1:28; II Corinthians 13:5, 6, 7; II Timothy 3:8; Titus 1:16).

The Analytical Greek Lexicon defines *"adokimos"*:— "unable to stand test, rejected, refuse, worthless".[3]

Where King James Version translates "castaway", Revised Version (1881) has "rejected". GNB/RSV/NAS all have "disqualified".

I conclude that if we had only this verse before us and the normal use of words in mind we would be bound to interpret in a severe manner. *"Adokimos"* is a strong, harsh expression.

The Second Principle demands that we pay careful attention to context. In the interpretation of this text we have an example of the harm that can be done by unfortunate chapter divisions. We ought to read from 9:24 without stopping, right on to 10:12. Is not 10:5 an illustration of what Paul meant by the word "adokimos"?

We may conclude that an application of rules 1 and 2 leads us to conclude that in this passage too *"adokimos"* means "reprobate".

Our Fourth Principle requires that no passage may be interpreted in such a way as will bring it into conflict with the total teaching of scripture.

Here we have to hesitate because the total teaching of scripture includes "the final perseverance of the saints". A true believer, which Paul was, cannot become "reprobate" or "castaway". Many commentators, amongst them some eminent reformed scholars, have found this consideration overwhelming. Great emphasis is laid, rightly, upon the necessity of paying heed to the context "Surely we must take all this into consideration, and not suddenly isolate the last verse".[4] But who says it is "the last verse?" We must not neglect the early part of chapter 10 which is also a part of the context.[5]

There are other passages in the New Testament, notably Hebrews 6:4–6 and 10:26–31 which apparently confront us with the same appalling possibility of falling away. Such passages have sometimes been interpreted as though they were hypothetical (i.e. situations which may be imagined for sake of argument but which can, in fact, never arise) and sermons have been preached which lay great emphasis upon the word "if" in Hebrews 6:6. There is nothing in the Greek to correspond with this word "if" however. It is dangerous to shrug off such solemn warnings by describing them as hypothetical or by supposing as some have done that they had reference only to Jewish Christians in the first century who were being tempted to revert to Judaism.

Both Scripture and church history suggest that it is possible for people to go very far in outward profession and even in what looks like spiritual attainment without ever being real believers.

Balaam, an Old Testament prophet, and Caiaphas, a New Testament prophet, both spoke remarkable words which correctly conveyed information about God's purposes but neither of them was a good man (Revelation 2:14; John 11:49—52). The Lord Himself in the Sermon on the Mount (Matthew 7:22, 23) warns us of the possibility of being successful preachers, evangelists, exorcists and miracle workers without ever being "known of God". Judas is clearly the most glaring example. Perhaps Demas is another (II Timothy 4:10).

And is it not highly probable that when Paul wrote about castaways he had in mind his own great but tragic ancestor, the first King of Israel, Saul the son of Kish of the tribe of Benjamin. Here was a man who started off with every advantage and upon whom, in some sense or another, the Spirit of God rested but from whom the Spirit is said to have departed. The recollection of this history, of the tragic reprobation of a man bearing his own name, will not permit us, as it cannot have permitted Paul, to write or to read the word "*adokimos*" without a thrill of horror. We dare not seek to bolster up the undoubted truth of the eternal security of the believer by watering down the powerful warnings that appear upon the pages of the New Testament. We work out our salvation with fear and trembling (Philippians 2:12) or by beating and buffeting (I Corinthians 9:27).

5.
Compare Scripture with Scripture

Rule Number Four requires us to *pay attention to the total teaching of the whole Bible; to compare Scripture with Scripture.*

Many New Testament passages can be understood only after reference to the Old Testament.

1. "Look, the Lamb of God, who takes away the sin of the world!" (John 1:29).

We must make use of the Epistle to the Hebrews to discover the parallels that the Holy Spirit intended us to draw out between the Old Testament sacrifices and the Lamb of God. The same epistle also instructs us in the differences between the old and the new and demonstrates the absolute superiority of Jesus Christ, the Lamb of God.

On the other hand, if we had only the New Testament John 1:29 and similar scriptures would leave us asking all sorts of puzzled questions as to what the expression "lamb of God" could mean and why a lamb should be necessary. The interpretation of the very difficult section of Ezekiel chapters 40—48 must be undertaken in the flood of light which the Hebrews epistle sheds upon the subject. The Hebrew epistle makes it inconceivable that there could ever be a restoration of the old sacrificial system either in whole or in part.

2. "You were redeemed . . . with the precious blood of Christ, a lamb without blemish or defect" (I Peter 1:18, 19).

For notes concerning "lamb" see the previous paragraph. To understand the words "without blemish" see Exodus 12 and Leviticus 1—5. To discover what is meant by the word "redeemed" we must turn to the Old Testament where we discover:

a. There is provision for the redemption of land (Leviticus 25:25—27).

b. There is provision for the redemption of houses (Leviticus 25:29).

c. There is provision for the redemption of slaves (Leviticus 25:47—49).

The book of Ruth provides us with a charming and very helpful illustration of the redemption which is in Christ Jesus for poor sinners. The near kinsman of Ruth and Naomi, named Boaz, redeemed the mortgaged family property and made Ruth his wife.

3. "Gird up the loins of your mind . . ." I Peter 1:13 (AV).

"And thus shall ye eat it; with your loins girded . . ." Exodus 12:11 (AV).

Just as the redeemed Israelites were to gird up their loins literally and address themselves to the long wilderness march to the promised land so the redeemed people of God are now to strip for action, discipline their minds, and set out on the journey through this world's wilderness to the heavenly Canaan. Even in countries where men (and even many women) wear trousers it should not be difficult to understand the expression "gird up the loins" but it is much easier for those who live in countries where long flowing garments are still the normal wear for men.

We must therefore beware of those who suggest that we could get along very well without the Old Testament. Those who are unfamiliar with the Old are going to find it very difficult to make sense of the New!

Beware of the danger of quoting the odd verse from here and there and building up some doctrine or theory upon it.

We must examine all the passages which have any bearing upon the matter. (It is also not at all uncommon to quote selectively from human authors!) The Jews were guilty of treating their scriptures in this way:

1. "We have heard from the Law that the Christ will remain for ever: so how can you say 'The Son of Man must be lifted up'?" These Jews found the assurances of Isaiah 9:7 and Daniel 7:14 very much to their taste because they fitted into their scheme of things but they were not prepared to give equal credence and value to other passages of scripture which taught or implied that the Son of man must be "lifted up", must suffer and die upon a tree, e.g. Isaiah 53:4—6; 53:12 and Daniel 9:26. These apparently self-contradictory prophecies have both been remarkably fulfilled in Jesus Christ. It should be noted that not only the enemies of Christ but His disciples too failed to understand and to interpret the Old Testament scriptures properly.

2. "How can the Christ come from Galilee? Does not the Scripture say that the Christ will come from David's family and from Bethlehem . . .?" (John 7:41, 42 Also see 7:52).

These cavillers who knew Micah 5:2 so well had apparently neglected to give due attention to Isaiah 9:1, 2 (quoted in Matthew 4:15, 16). It was true, of course, that Christ was to be born in Bethlehem; but it was also true that Christ was to come from Galilee and was to be a great light for the people of that province who sat in darkness.

Attention paid to parallel passages will often help us in the interpretation of scripture

Verbal parallels
For the discovery of verbal parallels a concordance is of

course invaluable; for the discovery of parallel passages dealing with any particular subject or subjects a topical concordance may be of value.[1]

a. David is called "a man after God's own heart" (I Samuel 13:14 and Acts 13:22). We may wonder what this could possibly mean. Similar words used in I Samuel 2:35 in a different connection will help us. "And I will raise up for myself a faithful priest, who will do according to what is in my heart and mind . . .". A man after God's own heart, therefore, is one who consciously conducts himself according to God's will and is faithful in the fulfilling of the duties assigned him by God.

b. "I bear on my body the marks of Jesus" (Galatians 6:17). What were these marks? Could they really have been the stigmata or marks of the nails as some Roman Catholics have imagined? We find a similar phrase in II Corinthians 4:10 "We always carry around in our body the death of Jesus". Further comparison with the passages II Corinthians 11:23—27 suggests that the "marks of Jesus" are the scars of the many beatings and floggings that Paul had suffered for Christ's sake.

Parallelism of Ideas:

a. "Drink ye all of it" Matthew 26:27 (AV)
    "Drink from it, all of you (NIV)

All those present on this occasion were apostles; does this command mean therefore that only priests should partake of the cup as the Roman church teaches? Look at the parallel passages. "For whenever you eat this bread and drink this cup . . . whoever eats the bread or drinks the cup of the Lord . . . A man ought to examine himself, before he eats of the bread and drinks of the cup" (I Corinthians 11:26, 27 and 28). Geoff. B. Wilson comments on verse 27: "This verse condemns the Romish practice of withholding the cup from the laity"[2] and then quotes L. Boettner as saying: "How could anyone be guilty of drinking the cup of the Lord in an unworthy manner if the cup were not given to him?"[3]

Incidentally, an ambiguity in the common English translations has led some people to suppose the command was
to drink up all the "consecrated" wine! Even a slight
knowledge of Greek in which there is no ambiguity would
prevent anyone falling into this error.

b. "You are Peter, and on this rock I will build my
church" (Matthew 16:18).

L. Boettner writes: "In the Greek the word Peter is
"Petros", a person, masculine, while the word rock is
"petra", which is feminine and refers not to a person
but to the declaration of Christ's deity that Peter had
just uttered — "You are the Christ, the Son of the living
God" . . . Had Christ intended to say that the Church
would be founded on Peter, it would have been ridiculous
for Him to have shifted to the feminine form of the word
in the middle of the statement . . . Clearly it was upon the
truth that Peter had expressed, the deity of Christ, and not
upon weak **vacillating** Peter that the church would be
founded . . . The Bible tells us plainly, not that the Church
has been built upon Peter, but that it is "built on the
foundation of the apostles and prophets and Christ Jesus
himself as the chief corner stone" (Ephesians 2:20). And
again, "For no one can lay any foundation other than the
one already laid, which is Jesus Christ" (I Corinthians
3:11)".[4]

In the Old Testament God Himself is repeatedly referred
to as the rock upon which His people are built (Deuteronomy 32:4, 15, 18; Psalm 18:2) and in the New Testament
Jesus Christ is repeatedly referred to as the rock upon
which the Church is built (Isaiah 28:16; I Peter 2:4–8;
Romans 9:33; I Corinthians 3:11).

c. "What counts is a new creation" (Galatians 6:15).
What is meant here by "a new creation"? Look up other
passages in which the words which precede this expression:
"Neither circumcision nor uncircumcision means anything" occur. Galatians 5:6 has these words and then
follows up with "but faith expressing itself by love". So

the man who is truly a new creature is characterised by a lively faith which works, and whose works are motivated by love. Then again I Corinthians 7:19 has "Circumcision is nothing and uncircumcision is nothing. Keeping God's commands is what counts". So a man who is a new creature is a man who keeps God's commandments.

d. "Love covers over a multitude of sins" I Peter 4:8 (NASB). Some have twisted this verse to mean that if they are lovingly disposed to everybody then their sins will somehow be cancelled out. But comparison with the parallel passage in Proverbs 10:12 should make it clear that whereas hatred stirs up trouble and tells tales, love is concerned to cover up another's sins and not to gossip about them. The love spoken of in the New Testament reference is a love which covers up other people's sins, not one's own sins.

Parallel histories

a. *In the Old Testament* We have two separate accounts of the period covered by the Jewish monarchy from David to the captivity — some 400 years:

  i. The two books of Kings together with the books of Samuel appear to have been written by prophets with the intention of recounting the history of kingship both in Israel and in Judah. The books of Kings begin with Solomon in all his glory and end with his descendant Jehoiachin a prisoner in exile.

  Of the 19 kings who ruled over Judah only 8 are said to have done that which was right in the sight of the Lord. Of the 19 kings who ruled over Israel (there were 9 different dynasties) all are said to have done that which was evil in the sight of the Lord.

  ii. The two books of Chronicles are concerned not so much with the history of the people or the history of their kings but to relate the history of the temple. The books were probably compiled by priests rather than by prophets and it has been supposed that perhaps Ezra who was both priest and scribe had a great deal to do with this compilation.

This limited priestly purpose in writing would explain why there is very little mention of the schismatical kingdom of Israel — they had rejected the divinely appointed temple, priesthood and sacrificial system. These books begin with the preparation for (I Chronicles) and the construction of (II Chronicles 1—7) Solomon's temple. They end with the decree of Cyrus to permit the building of a new temple to replace Solomon's which had been destroyed and burnt.

b. *In the Gospels* There are four gospels. They are not biographies or lives of Christ but all set out to relate some parts of his three years' ministry leading up to his death and resurrection. Only two (Matthew and Luke) relate the narratives connected with his birth and childhood. The first three gospels cover a great deal of the same ground; there is very little in John's gospel which can be found in the other three. There is only one miracle that is common to all four gospels and that is the miracle of the feeding of the 5,000. And, of course, the events of the last week of our Lord's life, of His death and of His resurrection, not only find a place in all four accounts but they occupy in all four what would be a completely disproportionate amount of space on the supposition that Christ's death was not much different from that of any other great man. Some examples of how to compare gospel with gospel are given below:—

i. Why did our Lord hurry the disciples off across the sea of Galilee after the feeding of the 5,000 when He must have known a dangerous storm was brewing? The gospels of Matthew and Mark inform us that he sent them off urgently while He withdrew to a hill top for prayer (Matthew 14:21; Mark 6:45). But they do not tell us why. John's gospel makes it clear that the well fed people were inclined to lead a political revolt against Rome and make Jesus their king (John 6:15). Jesus knowing that His foolish disciples might very well be carried away by this mood of excitement sent them out of danger (even though it meant sending them into another sort of danger) while he quietened the mob and dispersed them.

So if you plan to preach from any passage in any of the gospels it is wise always to discover if your text has parallel accounts in any or all of the other gospels and if so compare them carefully before committing yourself to any particular line of interpretation. A harmony of the gospels may help you in this particular type of study but many editions of the Bible very helpfully indicate in their margins where you may find the parallel passages.

ii. The Seven Sayings of Jesus from the Cross. Most people, with a little thought, could probably make a list of these, but very few would know where and in what gospels they were to be found. Luke reports three of the sayings and John reports a different three. "My God, my God, why have you forsaken me?", the fourth saying, is found in the two gospels, Matthew and Mark, and is the only one of the seven to appear in more than one of the gospels.

iii. The Resurrection Appearances. The ten different appearances are scattered here and there in the four gospels, in the book of the Acts and in I Corinthians 15.

The probable order of these appearances:—

1. to Mary Magdalene (Mark 16:9—11; John 20: 11—18)
2. to other Women (Matthew 28:9—10)
3. to Simon Peter (Luke 24:33—35; I Corinthians 15:5)
4. to two Disciples on road to Emmaus (Mark 16: 12—13; Luke 24:13—32)
5. to 10 Apostles and some other disciples (Mark 16:14; Luke 24:36—43; John 20:19—25)

All the above noted five appearances were on the very day of Resurrection — the first Easter Sunday.

6. to 11 Apostles including Thomas (John 20:26—29; 1 Corinthians 15:5)

7. to 7 Apostles beside Sea of Galilee (John 21:1–25)
8. to more than 500 brethren at once (Mark 16: 15–18; Matthew 28:16–20; I Corinthians 15:6)
9. to James the Lord's brother (I Corinthians 15:7)
10. Ascension (Luke 24:44–53; Acts 1:3–12; Mark 16:19–20)

c. *Parallel histories in the Acts*
   i. The conversion of Paul. This history is related three times:— Acts 9:1–22; 22:1–21; 26:1–20
   ii. The travels and Ministry of Paul. There is only one historical account and that is Luke's as we have it in the Acts of the Apostles. But scattered throughout the epistles are all sorts of allusions, many of them quite undesigned, which help to throw light upon and to confirm the accuracy of the account that Luke has left us.

The total teaching of Scripture

It is a fundamental rule of interpretation that we must not so interpret any passage of scripture (especially any obscure passage) in such a way as plainly to contradict the overall doctrinal thrust of the whole Bible. For example there are numerous passages which ascribe to God bodily parts and passions. We must not interpret these in such a way as to contradict the unambiguous and plain statement made by Jesus Himself in John 4:24, "God is Spirit". These anthropomorphic expressions, as they are called, are concessions to our human limitations of thought; if God did not condescend to speak of Himself as though he had bodily parts and passions we should find it very much harder, perhaps impossible, to comprehend Him and what He is saying.

6.
Figurative language

In the first five chapters of this book we have examined certain basic rules or principles which must be observed when attempting to interpret Scripture. These are fundamental principles which must apply to the whole of the Bible. However, there are many parts of scripture which are not written in ordinary straightforward language but in some form or another of figurative language, for the interpretation of which special considerations, over and above the rules thus far laid down, will need to be observed. Under this heading we will consider metaphor, parable, prophecy, symbolic language and types. The remainder of this book will be devoted to these matters. When the word "figure" is used in rhetoric it is defined as "a deviation from the ordinary mode of expression".[1] The word "trope" is defined as "a figure of speech, properly one in which a word or expression is used in other than its literal sense" or as "a figure of speech in which words are turned aside from their strict literal meaning".[2]

Metaphorical language

A simile is the explicit statement of some point of resemblance conceived to exist between two things, that differ in other respects. A metaphor is a potential or implied simile. In a simile both sides of the comparison are distinctly stated; whereas in a metaphor one side is stated, but not the other. If we say: "The Lord is like the sun" we are using simile. If we say: "The Lord is a sun" we are using metaphor. Some examples are set out below:—

1. "The Lord God is a sun and shield" (Psalm 84:11). He brings light and life to us as the sun does to the earth and its inhabitants; at the same time He is like a shield in that He protects His people from harm.

2. "The Lord is my rock, my fortress . . . my shield, and the horn of my salvation, my stronghold" Psalm 18:2

3. "The Lion of the tribe of Judah, the Root . . . " Revelation 5:5

4. "Look, the Lamb . . ." John 1:29

5. In John's gospel the Lord speaks of Himself as Bread, Light, a Door, a Shepherd, a Vine.

6. "Let the dead bury their own dead" Luke 9:60
"The first word 'dead' in this expression means 'the spiritually dead', the second the 'naturally dead'" says J. C. Ryle.[3]

7. "It is hard for you to kick against the goads" Acts 26:14
Ploughmen when using the primitive ploughs of ancient days used goads, sticks with sharp metal points, to urge on their oxen. Such goads are still used today in India by ploughmen and by ox-cart drivers. Saul's awakened conscience had been pricking him like the ploughman's ox-goad and he had been resisting and kicking against the protests of his conscience as some oxen kick against the goad. Such kicking only makes life worse for the oxen; and Saul's fighting against conscience only made him a more and more unhappy man.

8. "This is my body . . . this is my blood" Mark 14: 22, 24
At the time when these words were uttered the Lord's body had not been broken nor had His blood been shed. They must therefore be regarded as metaphorical language; it is wrong to interpret them literally. What our Lord is saying is "This bread is like my body which is to be broken for you; this wine is like my blood which is to be shed for many" just as when He says "I am the true vine . . ." He means that He is in some respects like a vine.

Symbolic language

Some examples of symbolic language are set out in tabular form below:—

Symbolic Expressions	Their Meaning	References
Earthquake storm and eclipse	Political upheaval	Isaiah 13:10–13; Jeremiah 4:23, 28; Joel 3:15; Matthew 24:29
Dew; Showers of rain; streams	Spiritual Blessing	Ezekiel 34:26; Hosea 14:5
Rod	Punishment	Isaiah 10:5; 14:29; I Corinthians 4:21
Marriage	God's covenant relationship with His people.	Hosea 2:19, 20
Adultery	Idolatrous breach of covenant made with God	
Wild Animals; Birds of prey; Horns	Great powers	Daniel 7; Zechariah 1:18, 19

Some symbolic expressions may have two different meanings, indeed two opposite meanings. One must decide upon the meaning intended in any particular passage by reference to the context. For example:

HARVEST	In some contexts "harvest" denotes the gathering in of converts (Matthew 9:37; John 4:35—38). In other contexts "harvest" denotes the reaping of what is ripe for judgement (Revelation 14: 14, 20).
FIRE	Burning up what is evil (Amos 1:4, 7, 10 etc; Hebrews 12:29). Judgement and Hell (Matthew 13:50; Luke 16:23, 24), or: Refining and Purifying of the Lord's people (Isaiah 6:6; Malachi 3:3; I Peter 1:7), or: Fire sometimes denotes the Holy Spirit and His work (Acts 2:3, 4; Luke 3:16).
LEAVEN	Secretly spreading evil (Mark 8:15; I Corinthians 5:8), or: Secretly and silently spreading good (Matthew 13:33).

But it should be noted that many Bible teachers insist that leaven should be interpreted consistently throughout the Bible of evil.[4]

Anthropomorphic language *(i.e. language which ascribes to God bodily parts)*

Although God is Spirit and so without body, parts or passions Scripture often speaks of Him, and indeed, represents God as speaking of Himself, as though He had both bodily parts and feelings.

"Surely the arm of the Lord is not too short to save, nor His ear too dull to hear" (Isaiah 59:1).

"I will guide thee with mine eye" Psalm 32:8 (AV).

"Such people are smoke in my nostrils" (Isaiah 65:5).

"Your arm is endued with power; your hand is strong, your right hand exalted" (Psalm 89:13).

"It is true that the Bible speaks of the hands and feet, the eyes and ears, the mouth and nose of God, but in doing this it is speaking anthropomorphically or figuratively of Him who far transcends our human knowledge and of whom we can only speak in a stammering fashion after the manner of men".[5]

Anthropopathic language *(i.e. language which ascribes to God human feelings and emotions)*

God's purposes are eternal and cannot change; He cannot change His mind. But in God's dealings with men there are apparent changes of course which are described as though they arose from God's disappointment with what He had done previously.

"It repented the Lord that he had made man on the earth, and it grieved him at his heart" Genesis 6:6 (AV).

"Let me alone, so that my anger may burn against them, and that I may destroy them . . ." Exodus 32:10 (AV).

"The Lord repented of the evil which he thought to do unto his people" Exodus 32:14 (AV).

"The Lord repented that he had made Saul king over Israel" I Samuel 15:35 (AV).

We deliberately retain the AV in this paragraph with its use of the puzzling word "repentance" in reference to God. Be careful to compare the passages set out above with those noted below so that your interpretation may be consistent with the total teaching of scripture.

"The Strength of Israel will not lie nor repent: for he is not a man, that he should repent" I Samuel 15:29 (AV).

"God is not man, that he should lie; neither the son of man, that he should repent . . ." Numbers 23:19 (AV).

7.
Parables

It is a common mistake to think that parables are delightful stories which can be easily understood by children. It is of course true that the parables are delightful stories and it is also true that they are capable of attracting the attention of both old and young. But it is by no means always a simple matter to discern their spiritual teaching.

In a parable the teacher aims to lead the disciple from the known to the unknown; from the familiar facts of every-day life to the unknown principles of the kingdom of heaven.

Note the reason why Jesus used the parabolic method (Matthew 13:11—17). "Why do you speak to the people in parables? He replied, The knowledge of the secrets of the kingdom of heaven has been given to you, but not to them".

What are the principles to guide our interpretation of parables?

1. Usually a parable is intended to teach ONE important lesson. Only a few parables (e.g. the parable of the sower and the parable of the tares) appear to teach more than one lesson. How may we discover what this one principle point is?

a. Sometimes it may be discovered in the introduction to the parable:

Luke 18:1—8 "They should always pray and not give up" is what the following story teaches.

Luke 18:9—14 The object of this story was to rebuke those who were confident of their own righteousness. But notice that the purpose of this parable is repeated, though in a slightly different way in the concluding verse.

Luke 19:11—27 One important purpose of this parable

was to teach that the kingdom of God was not to appear immediately.

b. Sometimes the object of the teacher is revealed only at the end of the parable:

Matthew 22:1–14 The final verse, "Many are invited but few are chosen", gives us the clue to the major purpose of this parable. Perhaps II Peter 1:10 is relevant.

Matthew 25:1–13 Again, it is the final verse which indicates the primary purpose of the parable: "Therefore keep watch, because you do not know the day or the hour".

Luke 16:1–9 What is virtually the final verse of this most difficult of all parables provides us with the clue: "Make to yourselves friends of the mammon of unrighteousness" (16:9 AV). "Use worldly wealth to gain friends for yourselves" (NIV). Some of our Lord's disciples had, like Matthew, been engaged in unworthy occupations and had amassed considerable fortunes by dishonest means (see Luke 15:1). When the question arose as to how this corrupt money was to be used Jesus told this parable. Two ways of solving the problem arise, if not clearly from the parable itself, then certainly from examples in following chapters.

i. If possible, make restitution to the person or persons who have been defrauded. ("I will pay back four times the amount" – Luke 19:8).

ii. If this should not be possible then the money should be distributed to the poor (Luke 18:22 and 19:8 "the half of my goods I give to the poor"). Or, in other words, by this wise use of fortunes made by dubious means make to yourselves friends. When the unjust steward called his master's debtors one by one and adjusted their accounts it is not likely that he was adding one more fraud to the many already perpetrated, for then his master would scarcely have commended him. It is more likely that he was dipping into his own ill gotten reserves and using some of them in such a way as to benefit immediately his old business associates and, in the long run, himself.

By way of example, let us suppose that some one before his conversion has hit the jackpot on the football pools or made a lot of money in some dubious business deal. Upon conversion or, perhaps more likely, some while after conversion he becomes uneasy about the way in which his money was gained. He may perhaps be able to return some or all of the money, perhaps with interest, to the government or institution or person defrauded. If that proves impossible, quixotic or dangerous, then perhaps the money may be used for educational and medical research. As to whether such monies should be accepted by Christian bodies for the Lord's work opinions may differ.

An interesting illustration of how this dilemma may be handled can be found in the fairly recent history of evangelicalism in this country. In the latter half of the 19th century there was a man named F. N. Charrington who belonged to the well known brewing family. Even after conversion he continued for some time enjoying the fortune which flowed to him from his family's brewing interests. But one night he observed some distressing sights outside a public house in London's East End and was particularly indignant at the abuse and blows that drunken husbands heaped upon their poor wives who were pleading with their husbands for money to buy food. He glanced up to see to whom the public house belonged and was considerably taken aback to see his own family name. He immediately sold all his interests in the family business and used the proceeds to finance a vigorous work for religious and social reform amongst the poor of the East End of London.

c. Sometimes the teacher's object is stated at the beginning of the parable and then repeated at the end, usually in different words:
Matthew 18:21, 22 "you are to forgive not seven times only but until seventy times seven."

Matthew 18:35 "This is how my heavenly Father will treat each of you unless you forgive your brother from your heart."

Luke 12:15 "Watch out! Be on your guard against all kinds of greed . . . and He told them this parable . . ."

Luke 12:21 "This is how it will be with anyone who stores up things for himself but is not rich towards God".

d. Sometimes we are to discover the primary purpose of a parable by reference to the context and to the circumstances in which the parable was told:

Luke 13:6—9 In the preceding verses 3 and 5 "Unless you repent, you too will all perish", and then the parable of the fruitless fig tree is told.

    The fig tree = Jewish nation
    The master   = God's Justice (ready to smite)
    The gardener = God's longsuffering "the long-suffering of God waited" (I Peter 3:20)

We may now apply this parable to some churches and individuals. Any tree that in spite of continued care, digging and dunging, fails to produce fruit will one day be suddenly cut down without remedy (cf. Proverbs 29:1).

Note: We must not, when interpreting this parable, make the master mean God and the gardener mean Jesus. This would land us in all sorts of theological muddle and in a very unscriptural mis-representation of the relationship between the persons of the Trinity in the work of salvation.

Luke 15:12—32 Read the first two verses of the chapter. "Then drew near unto him all the publicans and sinners for to hear him. And the Pharisees and the scribes murmured . . ." (AV). It was to counter this murmuring that Jesus told the parable (see 15:3), the threefold parable that follows.

    The younger son = a publican/sinner
    The elder son   = pharisee/scribe

2. We saw earlier that a parable is generally told to teach one particular lesson. In interpreting parables we should make it our business to discover that one over-riding consideration and see that we make the parable teach that, and perhaps only that, to those whom we are instructing. There are two reasons for not trying to attach meaning to all the details that fill out the parabolic story. The first and more important is that we shall probably be inventing meanings for the minutiae of the story that the Story-Teller Himself never intended. The second is that pre-occupation with the minutiae, even should our interpretation succeed in avoiding the fanciful, invariably leads to an obscuring of the primary purpose of the parable. Or, in other words, we shall be unable to see the wood for the trees.

For example, it is unnecessary and dangerous to try and discover meanings for the ring, shoes and fatted calf of the Lord's best known and best loved parable. Our Lord was a master of the art of telling short stories and in spite of the astonishing brevity of most of his stories he was able to fill them out with a large number of attractive little touches which help to bring the picture vividly before the eyes of the mind.

However, having said that, I must confess that I delight to think of the "best robe" as being a picture of the imputed righteousness of Christ, the wedding garment of Matthew 22:1–14, and the robe of righteousness of Isaiah 61:10.

Let us look at the parable of The Good Samaritan. The main thrust of this story, perhaps the only thrust, is to teach the duty of showing a helpful neighbourly spirit to all who are in trouble regardless of such distinctions as may arise from race, colour or creed. But some, possibly to escape the harsh challenge "Go and do likewise" turn the parable into an illustration of the gospel. Once you start on that slippery slope in no time at all the inn becomes the church, the two pence the two sacraments and the promised return of the Samaritan the second advent of Christ! J. C. Ryle deals in very forthright and characteristic fashion with this dubious way of handling the parables.[1]

3. We must not seek to establish any doctrine solely upon the basis of a parable.

For example, we may not argue from the prayer made by the rich man in hell to father Abraham that prayers directed to saints in glory are the teaching of scripture. Such a conclusion would be out of harmony with the plain teaching of the rest of scripture.

Many liberals conclude from the fact that the prodigal son was pardoned and received the moment he returned home without any mention of sacrifice and atonement that, in the preaching of the gospel, it is not necessary to speak of Christ as the sin bearer and of His precious blood as the price of our redemption. But such a "simple" gospel which disregards God's wrath against sin and the necessity for a satisfaction to be made to Divine Justice runs counter to the plain straightforward teaching of all the epistles. In the very nature of the case a parable cannot cram within itself all those features which go to make up the total way of salvation — it was never intended to do so. It highlights in a dramatic and most effective manner some one or two features only. To take these one or two features and turn them into the whole of salvation's plan is a very dishonest way of handling scripture.

4. Do not take some detail of a parable and make it the foundation of an important teaching.

For instance, are we to conclude that because five virgins were wise and five foolish that only half of all professing Christians will go into the marriage supper while half will be rejected? Or, because in the parable of the sower there are four different soils only one of which produced a crop are we to conclude that three quarters of all gospel seed sowing proves unproductive? Nor is there any special significance in the fact that one of ten coins and one of a hundred sheep were lost.

Allegory

If parable is extended simile then allegory is extended metaphor. Although John's gospel has no parables it does use allegory in chapters 10 and 15. It may be instructive to set out the details of these allegories in one column with the interpretation given of them in a parallel column.

Allegorical details	*Interpretation*
shepherd	Jesus said: "I am the good shepherd"
sheep	
gate-keeper	
fold	
door	"I am the door" John 10:7 & 9
robbers	"all that came before me" 10:8
strangers	
wolf	
hireling	

Note that surprisingly few of the details of this allegory are positively identified by the Lord Jesus Himself. The sheep must clearly represent the Lord's believing people but with reference to other details there may be uncertainty and indeed it may not be necessary for us to seek interpretation of every point.

In John 15 we may list the following:—

the vine	Jesus said: "I am the true vine"
husbandman	Jesus said: "My Father is the . . ."
branches	"You are the branches"

Care has to be taken in interpreting this passage to accommodate, in a way consistent with the rest of scripture, the difficult passage about the fruitless branches that are cut away, cast out, and burned. For those who believe we may be saved one day and lost the next there is no problem. We who are sure that "the final perseverance of saints" is a scriptural doctrine are tempted to torture the passage into a conformity with our doctrine. We must avoid doing this; a satisfactory and satisfying exposition of this admittedly difficult passage may be found in Hendriksen's Commentary on John's Gospel.[2]

There are some allegories to be found in the Old Testament, as for example Judges 9:8—15 (or is this more properly a fable?); Psalm 80:8—16; Proverbs 5:15—18 and Ecclesiastes 12:3—7.

8.
Types

Some persons whom we meet in the Old Testament, some religious festivals and acts of religious worship, some historical events and some things, are types; that is to say they provide us with a foreshadowing of the reality that is revealed in the New Testament. They were, and were intended to be, "figures of the true" (Hebrews 9:24).

"The great rule of interpretation is to ascertain the scope of an allegory either by reference to the context, or to parallel passages; and to seize the main truth which it is intended to set forth, interpreting all accessories in harmony with the central truth.

"Some expositors have unwarrantably turned histories into allegories disregarding the distinction between legitimate illustrations arising out of the narratives, and a mystical rendering of the whole as a fable . . . Thus the journey of Eliezer to Padan-aram to seek a wife for Isaac contained not only an interesting fact in the patriarchal history, with important moral lessons founded on the readiness of the maiden to leave a land of idolaters to cast in her lot with the Chosen People; but an allegory of the Divine Father commissioning His Spirit to go forth into the world to win a Bride for His Son.

"Such applications, indeed, sometimes vindicate themselves by their appositeness." However, "it cannot be too clearly borne in mind that the INTERPRETATION OF AN ALLEGORY is one thing, ALLEGORICAL INTERPRETATION quite another".[1]

As an illustration of the unbridled fancifulness to which allegorical interpretation may lead, Angus in a footnote supplies the following on I Samuel 13:1 "Saul was a child of one year when he began to reign, and he reigned two years over Israel." The Douai version thus comments: "That is, he was good, and like an innocent child, and for two years continued in that innocency".[2]

There are two opposite views with respect to the subject of typology. The first is that we should consider as types only those which are referred to as such in the New Testament; that is, there must be clear divine sanction before we regard any person or thing or event as having typical significance. The other view which goes to the opposite extreme is to regard almost everything in the Old Testament as having typical meaning with the result that people become obsessed with the subject and bring a great deal of imaginative ingenuity to the discovery of typical significance in every hook, tent peg and socket of the tabernacle. The writer thinks that the first position is probably a trifle too conservative and that where the parallel of Old Testament fact and New Testament reality is so clear that it could not be by chance, the Old Testament fact may be regarded as typical even if it is not directly asserted to be so.

We can expect to find typical resemblance only in some matters; if we strain to find them in all we shall fall into error. Moreover an abuse of typology will rob us of the many blessed lessons that arise out of the plain historical interpretation of the sacred text.

Typical persons

a. *Adam:* Constituted head of the human race. *Christ:* (the last Adam) constituted head of the redeemed people of God, the new humanity. Romans 5:14 gives clear sanction to our regarding Adam as a type of Christ: "who was a pattern of the one to come." (Also I Corinthians 15:22, 45).

b. *Joseph:* There is no direct New Testament sanction for calling Joseph a type of Christ but the parallels between his history and that of Jesus Christ are so many and so

exact that many would conclude that Joseph and his
experiences were intended by the Holy Spirit to be an
illustration of New Testament reality.

Joseph was hated of his brethren but finally became
ruler of Egypt and the "saviour" of his people and of the
world (Acts 7:9—13). Jesus came unto His own and His
own received Him not (John 1:11) but He became universal ruler and the Saviour of both Jews and Gentiles.

c. *Moses:* The great prophet of his people who told them
that in due course: "God will raise up for you a prophet
from among your own brothers, like me" (Deuteronomy
18:15—19). Also see Acts 3:22, 23; 7:35.

d. *Aaron:* As the first High Priest was typical of Christ
in his high priestly work (Hebrews 5:1—5; 10:21).

e. *Melchizedek:* Aaron could typify only the earthly
aspects of the high priestly work of Christ. Melchizedek
sets forth the heavenly work of Jesus, the One who ever
lives to make intercession. Aaron was priest only and
could not be a king. Melchizedek was a king, a priest-
king, and so could typify Christ in the exercise of this
dual role (Hebrews 5:6—10; 6:20; 7:1—25).

f. *Joshua:* What Moses could not accomplish Joshua
was raised up to do, namely, to bring redeemed Israel
into the promised land. And so "what the law could not
do" was accomplished through God's Son who not only
brings us from out of bondage but also brings us to glory.

g. *David:* The ideal king who overcame all his enemies
and devoted the spoil to the erection of a temple for an
habitation of God is a remarkable type of our king Jesus
who "must reign until he has put all his enemies under
his feet" (I Corinthians 15:25) and who as the result of
His Calvary/Resurrection triumph is able to equip His
church with all the gifts necessary to the completion of
"a holy temple in the Lord" (Ephesians 2:20—22).

h. *Solomon:* Solomon was David's son; Messiah was
great David's greater Son. Solomon typifies our Lord
Jesus as "prince of Peace"; he built a magnificent house

of stone and cedar wood while Jesus builds a glorious church of "living stones", "a holy temple in the Lord" (Matthew 16:18; Ephesians 2:20—22).

Caution It must constantly be borne in mind that persons in the Old Testament who may be regarded as types of Christ are typical only in some aspects of their lives and characters and *not in all.*

Adam was typical of Christ in respect of the fact that he was constituted head of the human race. He was not typical of Christ when yielding to temptation. Moses was a remarkable prophet, the deliverer of his people from bondage and faithful in all God's house (Hebrews 3:1—6). In these ways he was a remarkable foreshadowing of Christ; but he was clearly not like our Lord when he spake unadvisedly with his lips. So we must expect to find typical resemblance only in some matters; if we strain to find them in all we shall fall into error.

The religious feasts of the Hebrew religion were types
a. *Sabbath:* This sets before us the heart rest which arises from a blessed assurance of salvation, and also the eternal rest of heaven.
b. *Passover:* "For even Christ our passover" (I Corinthians 5:7).
c. *Old Testament sacrifices:* Although not "the realities themselves" (NIV) they were "a shadow of good things to come" (Hebrews 10:1).

The anointed ministries of the Old Testament were typical
There were three kinds of people who were solemnly anointed to hold office: prophets, priests and kings. The Lord Jesus combined all three offices within His own glorious person and work. He was:
    a. Prophet, Rabbi (Guru) and Teacher.
    b. Priest, Redeemer. Intercessor.
    c. King, Lord.

It is important when preaching the gospel to proclaim Christ in all His offices. It is not sufficient that new converts should be instructed to receive Christ as Saviour, or as Saviour and Friend. They must be taught to embrace "a whole Christ", to receive Him as Saviour, Teacher and Lord.

Many of the historical events connected with Israel were typical

"Jewish history and worship form one grand type . . . Their sufferings in Egypt, their deliverance under Moses, their wanderings in the desert, their entry into Canaan, prefigure important facts in the history of all Christians . . . the facts of their history were typical of the history of the Church (Romans 2:28; I Corinthians 10; Hebrews 4; I Peter 2:5—10; Revelation 15:5)".[3]

From the time that they set out from Egypt until they reached the promised land many of the things that happened to them such as the provision of daily manna and the provision of water from out of the smitten rock were a foreshadowing of the experiences of the redeemed people of God as they make their pilgrim progress to the Celestial City (I Corinthians 10:1—11).

The Brazen Serpent lifted up on a pole so that dying Israelites might look and live is a type, clearly sanctioned by our Lord Himself, of the Saviour lifted up upon the cross that whoever looks believingly to Him should not perish but have everlasting life (Isaiah 45:22; John 3: 14, 15).

Many articles connected with Jewish religious worship were types

This is particularly true of the tabernacle and its furniture much of which foreshadows various aspects of the person and work of the Lord Jesus Christ and of His relationship to His church. But it is doubtful if we are intended to attempt finding a typical meaning in every hook and tent peg. And even if such a mode of interpretation could be justified it would be deplorable if it were to obscure those lessons that are of major importance and that are clearly sanctioned by the New Testament. The Holy Spirit was showing by this, that the way into the Most Holy Place had not yet been disclosed as long as the first tabernacle was still standing. The message is "Keep out". But, "when Christ came" (Hebrews 9:8—11) and when the veil of His flesh was torn and the veil in the temple was at the same time rent from top to bottom the message changed from a warning "Keep out" to a welcoming "Let us draw near". (Hebrews 10:19—22)

9.
Prophecy

The nature of prophecy

The common impression is that this has to do with prediction and nothing else. However, the prophets spoken of in scripture were men who spoke forth a message for God and while undoubtedly a great deal of prophecy is predictive in character a very large part of the prophetic task consisted in speaking God's message to the people among whom they lived and to the situations in which they found themselves. They were "forth-tellers" more than they were "fore-tellers".

1. *Forth-telling:* The prophet's task was to listen to what God told him and then preach the message to the people. Aaron is said to have acted as Moses' prophet: "See, I have made you like God to Pharaoh, and your brother Aaron will be your prophet" (Exodus 7:1). Aaron did not deliver his own message but spoke out only those things that were communicated to him by his brother. True prophets heard what God the Lord communicated to them and then spoke it to the people and/or wrote it down.

The prophet Samuel established a school of the prophets where groups of young men called "the sons of the prophets" were presumably instructed in the Law, in church music and in other such matters. They lived together in little communities and Samuel travelled around to visit them and supervise their instruction (I Samuel 19:20; II Kings 4:1, 38; 6:1, 2). When godly kings reigned they often worked in close harmony with the prophets and consulted them with a view to learning what might be God's will. On the other hand when evil men occupied the throne the prophets were not only neglected but sometimes ill treated and even put to death. False and hireling prophets were encouraged and there seemed always to be plenty of that sort around (I Kings 22:6, 8; Jeremiah 14:14; 23:21). Some of the prophets became what are known as writing prophets and their writings, or at least some of them, make up a large part of our Old Testament. God would sometimes communicate his message directly to His servants, sometimes by dreams and visions. Moses was unique in that God spoke with him "face to face" (Deuteronomy 34:10). True prophets after they had received God's message in one or another of these ways, conscious of divine authority, were able to proclaim: "Thus saith the Lord . . .". Besides kings and priests, prophets also were sometimes, if not always, anointed with oil (I Kings 19:16) to signify that they had been set apart for this special task.

2. *Foretelling:* The predictive part of the prophet's task might involve him in foretelling such events as the deportation and captivity of God's people, their deliverance and return, their world-wide dispersion, the birth, life and death of the Messiah, His second advent and eternal kingdom.

The fulfilment of prophecy

It is not necessary to suppose that each prophecy has but one fulfilment. On the contrary, it seems quite evident that many prophetic utterances are susceptible of a double interpretation. They may have an immediate reference and an ultimate reference; a partial fulfilment and a complete fulfilment. We may append a few examples:—

1. "So shall your offspring be . . ." (Genesis 15:5).

The immediate and partial fulfilment was to be found in the remarkable growth of the Hebrew nation (Exodus 32: 13; Deuteronomy 1:10, 11).

The more distant and complete fulfilment is to be found in the world-wide expansion of the Christian church — the true "Israel of God" (Galatians 6:16 and also Galatians 3:8, 9). "Abraham . . . is the father of us all . . ." (Romans 4:16, 17).

2. "The sceptre will not depart from Judah . . ." (Genesis 49:10).

The immediate and partial fulfilment is found in the preservation of the Davidic kingship, in spite of Solomon, and in spite of the division of the kingdom (I Kings 11: 36), until the time of the deportation to Babylon. But the more distant and complete fulfilment is found in David's greater Son of whom it was said by the angel: "He will reign over the house of Jacob for ever; his kingdom will never end" (Luke 1:33).

3. "He is the one who will build a house for my Name, and I will establish the throne of his kingdom for ever. I will be his father, and he shall be my son" (II Samuel 7:13—15).

The immediate reference is, of course, to Solomon. But the ultimate reference is clearly to the Lord Jesus (see Luke 1:33) which reference is sanctioned by the way in which the Hebrews epistle quotes this passage: "I will be his Father, and He will be my son" (ch. 1:5). Note that the latter part of II Samuel 7:14 cannot possibly have any reference to the Lord.

4. Matthew 24. Some of the prophecies in this chapter refer to the destruction of Jerusalem which was to take place after 40 years in A.D. 70. Others would find fulfilment only in the events connected with our Lord's Return. Some may have a double reference, immediately to the destruction of Jerusalem and ultimately to the events connected with the end of the age. "Wherever there is a carcass, there the vultures will gather" (Matthew 24:28) may be susceptible of a threefold fulfilment.

a. When the Jewish religious society in the disastrous years following the rejection of the Messiah degenerated into a corpse-like condition the Roman armies descended upon that corpse, encamping round about the city, and finally tore it to pieces. An eagle was the symbol of Roman military might.

b. We have in this century seen a number of corrupt

"christian" societies lapse into such a moribund condition that the way has been opened up for atheistic and anti-god movements to descend like vultures upon the corpses and tear them apart.

c. At the end when this world's political systems and cultures have run themselves into the ground and have become so corrupt that they can no longer function the vultures first of anarchy and then of Armageddon may be expected to do their frightful work.

The figurative language of prophecy

(Reference may be made to paragraph 2 of chapter 6 under the heading "Symbolic Language"). P. 67.

Symbolic Expressions	Their Meaning	References
Sun Moon Stars	Great World Powers	Joel 2:10, 31
Cedars of Lebanon Ships of Tarshish	Wealthy Merchants	Isaiah 2:13; Ezekiel 31:3 Isaiah 2:16
Earth-quakes	Political Revolution	Zechariah 14:5 Revelation 6:12; 11:19; Isaiah 24:20

Darkening of sun and moon	The End of the World	Matthew 24:29; Acts 2:20; Isaiah 13:10; Revelation 6:12
Stars falling		Matthew 24:29; Revelation 6:12
Dew, Showers, Rain, Water, Rivers	Blessings connected with the outpouring of the Holy Spirit	Isaiah 44:3; Hosea 14:15; John 4:10; 7:38
Moab, Ammon, Edom, Babylon	Enemies surrounding and threatening the people of God (the church)	Isaiah chs. 13—23; Amos 1:1 to 2:3
The horn of David	Salvation that comes through the preaching of the Gospel. The Lord Jesus Christ	Psalm 132:17; Luke 1:75
King David	The Messiah, the Lord Jesus	Jeremiah 30:9; Ezekiel 34:24; 37:24; Hosea 3:5; Acts 13:34
Jerusalem, Zion	The church or God's kingdom	Isaiah 52:1—9; 60:1—14; Galatians 4:26; Hebrews 12:22
The prosperous days of David or Solomon	Messiah's reign (some would suggest — a millennial period of great earthly prosperity)	I Kings 4:25; Micah 4:4; Zechariah 3:10);

Some peculiarities of prophetic language

1. Things yet far in the future are sometimes spoken of as though they had already happened. For example:

"Unto us a child is born" (Isaiah 9:6)

"He was despised and rejected" (Isaiah 53:3, 4)

"He hath borne our griefs" (AV) and many more.

In this particular instance the events foretold were 800 years in the future and yet all the verbs used are in the past tense.

The use of verbs in the past tense, the so called prophetic perfect, in connection with things still in the future is a way of emphasising the certainty of those predictions being fulfilled. An interesting and profoundly encouraging example meets us in the well known passage Romans 8:30: "Those he predestined, he also called; those he called, he also justified; those he justified, he also glorified".

2. Two or more events which in their fulfilment may be separated by long periods of time are sometimes foretold, as though they belonged together, in one verse or paragraph of the prophetic scriptures.

a. "To proclaim the year of the Lord's favour and the day of vengeance of our God" (Isaiah 61:2).

When our Lord introduced Himself and His ministry to the people of Nazareth by reading this scripture from Isaiah he stopped abruptly after reading the words "favourable year of the Lord" closed the book and gave it to the attendant. In this way He made it clear that His immediate mission was to proclaim God's favour and mercy. "The favourable year" was already come; the "day of vengeance" still lay far in the future.

b. "I will pour out my Spirit in those days . . . the great and dreadful day of the Lord" (Joel 2:29–31).

According to Acts 2:16, 17 the first part of the passage quoted from Joel was fulfilled, or at least began to be fulfilled, at Pentecost. The great and awesome day of the Lord still lies in the future.

c. "See your king comes to you . . . Gentle and riding on a donkey . . . His rule will extend from sea to sea . . ." Zechariah 9:9, 10.

The first part of the quotation found its fulfilment on the Sunday we sometimes call Palm Sunday, the Sunday before the crucifixion. It emphasises the humiliation and unpretentiousness of our Lord's first advent. The latter part of the quotation speaks of the great glory of His universal kingdom. That lies still in the future.

10.
Prophecy (*continued*)

Some rules for the interpreting of prophetic scriptures

1. Find out as much as you can about the circumstances in which the prophet proclaimed his message.
2. Take care to interpret the prophet's use of figurative language correctly (see the previous chapter).
3. Before deciding upon the interpretation of any particular prediction discover if there are similar or parallel predictions elsewhere in the same prophet or in the writings of other Old Testament prophets. Parallel predictions will often throw light upon one another.

For example, there are no less than six passages which speak of Christ as the Branch, distributed between three different prophets.

a. In that day the Branch of the Lord will be beautiful and glorious (Isaiah 4:2).

b. A shoot will come up from the stump of Jesse; from his roots a Branch (Isaiah 11:1).

c. The days are coming . . . when I will raise up to David a righteous Branch (Jeremiah 23:5).

d. In those days . . . I will make a righteous Branch sprout from David's line (Jeremiah 33:15).

e. I am going to bring my servant, the Branch (Zechariah 3:8).

f. Here is the man whose name is the Branch (Zechariah 6:12).

4. Take great care to notice what predictions are fulfilled in the gospel story or in the story of the early church and notice the way and the circumstances in which they are fulfilled.
5. Study the way in which the Lord and His apostles interpreted Old Testament predictions and what use they

made of them. This is perhaps the most important rule of all. Do not forget that all these spake and wrote under inspiration of the Holy Spirit and their methods of interpretation are therefore inspired guidance for us to follow. It is worthwhile noting that for the most part they regard these Old Testament predictions as finding their fulfilment in the Christian church and its history.

Some examples
Joel 2: 28, 29 Peter quoting this passage on the day of Pentecost declares: "This is what was spoken by the prophet Joel . . ." (Acts 2:16, 17).
Amos 9: 11, 12 James in giving his judgment in the Jerusalem consultation about new Gentile converts says: The words of the prophets are in agreement with this (God's calling out from the Gentiles a people for himself) as it is written: "After this I will return, and rebuild David's fallen tent . . ." (Acts 15:16, 17).
Exodus 19:5, 6 Everything here that is spoken of God's people (Israel in the wilderness) is regarded by Peter as being true of the church (I Peter 2:9).
Hosea 2:23 What is spoken of Israel in this passage is spoken of the church by Peter in I Peter 2:10 and is specifically applied to Gentile believers in Romans 9:25.

Different ways in which prophetic scripture is interpreted

The spiritualising method
a. Not all of the prophecies are to be interpreted literally. The examples that we have looked at above of the way in which our Lord and His apostles quoted and used the Old Testament appear to support this view.
b. Some more extreme exponents of this spiritualising method maintain that there are now no prophecies respecting literal Israel that remain to be fufilled. Their time has gone forever; God has no further dealings with the Jewish

people as a race or nation. All the prophecies that appear to foretell great prosperity for the people of Israel are to find their fulfilment in the world wide planting and prosperity of the Christian church; Jews converted to Christ will take their place within this sphere of great spiritual prosperity and blessedness alongside of their Gentile fellow-believers.

However, the events of the past thirty years must surely give pause to the more dogmatic exponents of this view. The establishing, contrary to all reasonable expectations, of an Israeli State in Palestine using Hebrew as its national language, and the hitherto overwhelming success that this new and tiny nation has achieved against impossible odds surely have to be accommodated somehow, somewhere, in our interpretation both of scripture and history.

The literalist method
Wherever possible the prophetic scripture, like every other part of scripture, should be interpreted literally. A common slogan amongst such students of prophecy has been: "The Bible says what it means and means what it says". The whole argument, of course, turns on the phrase "wherever possible"! Some of those who take this view expect a literal rebuilding of Babylon and, on the basis of Ezekiel chapters 40—48, a literal rebuilding of the Jewish temple at Jerusalem and a resumption of many of the old sacrificial ceremonies. It was the absolute impossibility of reconciling such a view of things with the Epistle to the Hebrews that finally led the writer to suspect and then discard the pre-millennial views which he had more or less taken for granted from childhood.

After the removal of the church, it was supposed that God would resume His dealings with Israel and would bless them more and more and use them as an instrument of government and of evangelisation throughout a thousand years of unexampled earthly prosperity.

Some who reject the pre-millennial system, just briefly

outlined, look for a period of very great spiritual awakening and blessing which will include a large scale turning of Jews to the Lord, before the end of the world and the return of the Lord Jesus for His people (See Romans 11: 26). But do such scriptures as Matthew 24:12 and II Timothy 3:1 support such expectations?

One thing is certain: "it is not for you to know the times or dates the Father has set by His own authority" (Acts 1:7). Therefore any scheme of interpretation which includes date fixing is plainly unscriptural. Let us, in concluding, remember that our Lord Jesus Christ is Himself the focal point and end of all prophecy. Just as He fulfils within Himself all the law so He will fulfil and complete all prophecy. "The testimony of Jesus is the spirit of prophecy" (Revelation 19:10) which perhaps means that the whole driving force behind the utterance of true prophecy, the whole inspiring motive, is to testify concerning Jesus, to set Him securely at the centre. "And beginning with Moses and all the Prophets, He explained to them what was said in all the scriptures concerning Himself" (Luke 24:27). "Concerning this salvation, the prophets . . . searched intently . . . trying to find out the time and circumstances to which the Spirit of Christ in them was pointing when he predicted the sufferings of Christ and the glories that would follow." (I Peter 1:10, 11). "These are the Scriptures that testify about Me" (John 5:39; Acts 3:18, 24; 10:43; Romans 1:2; 3:2).

"Do not think that I have come to abolish the law, or the prophets; I have not come to abolish them but to fulfil them" (Matthew 5:17).

11.
On Hebrew poetry

A very large part of the Old Testament is written in poetical form so that it is essential for any would-be preacher and interpreter of the scriptures to know at least a little about the leading characteristics of Hebrew poetry. The chief formal characteristic of the psalms (and of other poetical sections of the Bible), the most obvious element of pattern, is, happily, one that survives in translation. It is the practice of saying the same thing twice in different words, which we call parallelism. A perfect example is:— The One enthroned in heaven laughs; the Lord scoffs at them (Psalm 2:4) or, The heavens declare the glory of God; the skies proclaim the work of his hands (Psalm 19:1).

This poetic parallelism admits of great variety so that there is little danger of the reader finding these parts of scripture tedious; there is no mechanical sameness about these poems. Moreover, this characteristic of Hebrew poetry is one which is not (like rhyme or metre) lost in translation. It can therefore be turned into all the languages of the world without loss of beauty or impressiveness and we can only conclude that God's providential ordering is manifest in this peculiarity of Hebrew language.

The most common form of parallelism is the one illustrated above where the second line does little more than re-echo the first, but in different words. Sometimes the second line amplifies the first; it says a little more than was in the first line. The first variety of parallelism is called "synonymous" whereas the second is called "synthetic". Of this latter take by way of example:—

> The Lord is my shepherd,
> I shall lack nothing. (Psalm 23:1)
> He makes me lie down in green pastures,
> he leads me beside quiet waters (Psalm 23:2)

Yet another variety of parallelism is called "antithetic" when the first and the second lines present contrasting ideas. This is particularly suitable to a book like Proverbs where in so many chapters we have set before us "moral virtues and their contrary vices" (to quote the heading provided in the AV). But there are many examples elsewhere as in Psalm 1:6—

"For the Lord watches over the way of the righteous, but the way of the wicked will perish." (NIV)[1]

An understanding of the parallelistic structure of Hebrew poetry is hermeneutically important for two reasons:—

1. Where the construction of one line may appear to us to be complicated we may find the parallel line sufficiently clear to enable us to determine the meaning of the complicated and ambiguous member.

This principle is sometimes of help to translators. On the other hand translators should be cautious. It is doubtful how far they are justified in conjectural emendations of the text because they think that parallelism demands emendations. They, and we, must always be prepared for irregularities (inspired irregularities!) in the poetical and parallelistic structure.

The Revised Standard Version which is in many respects an excellent modern translation appears to have been somewhat reckless in making corrections to the Hebrew text on these grounds. Serious readers should always read any preface which sets out the principles which have guided the translators in their work and they should always examine any footnotes that may be supplied e.g. RSV always indicates by the use of the abbreviation "Cn" (correction) when it has amended the Hebrew text. Be even more circumspect when using a translation or paraphrase which provides no footnote to alert the unwary reader! Students of Psalms and Proverbs would be well advised to consult Derek Kidner's Tyndale Old Testament Commentaries;[2] he repeatedly warns us as, for example, in Psalm 95:7 "The attractive variant in NEB . . . is only a network of conjectures"[3] or on Psalm 97:10 "RSV's alterations make a smoother sentence . . . But the textual support is scanty, AND SMOOTHNESS IS NOT A SAFE CRITERION"[4] (my capitals!).

However, nothing said here is intended to discourage the student from a judicious use of modern translations. The KJV may be more often right than some moderns will allow and more often wrong than some ultra-conservatives will admit.

The Good News Bible frequently ignores altogether the parallelistic structure of the poetical portions of scripture. It does not include the titles of the Psalms (except in footnotes) although these are part of the inspired text. RSV and NASB are far more reliable in these respects and the latter is particularly helpful in the way in which it sets out each separate line.

2. If this parallelistic pattern is not recognised we may fall into the trap of trying to get a different meaning out of each line of a verse where the same thing is being said in different words. Some rather odd interpretations have emerged as a result of neglecting this principle!

12.
Historical and cultural context

We have repeatedly insisted in earlier chapters that our interpretation must be governed by the three-fold biblical context of (i) the immediate passage, (ii) the scope of the book or section of scripture in which our text is found, and (iii) the analogy of faith, or the over-all teaching of the whole Bible. However, some writers on the subject of Interpretation insist upon another sort of three-foldness. For example Brian Edwards in his excellent book "Nothing But the Truth" writes: "Every word of the Bible has three contexts. We may think of these as the room, the house, and the street in which the word lives. The room is the biblical context . . . The house in which the biblical room is situated is the historical context . . . The street, in which the historical house contains the biblical room represents the local conditions of the day. This is the cultural context . . . The three contexts of every Biblical verse are the biblical room, the historical house and the street of local conditions. The first is essential; the other two are very helpful . . ."[1]

Some applications of this rule have been severely criticised on the grounds "that the Word of God was ALL written for ALL Christians in ALL ages". Providing this statement is not pressed to mean more than is said in II Timothy 3:16 no evangelical believer would dissent. But if it is so pressed we shall find ourselves saddled with a number of eccentric practices that are manifestly quite unsuited to our clime or culture. There are still to be found in some remote parts of the United States a sect dubbed "Hook and Eye Mennonites" who regard the use of buttons as being worldly. Also in the United States there are Free-Will Baptists who still practice feet-washing. And if all the Word of God is literally for all Christians in all ages then we might be required to stone adulterous men and women to death.

The writer while in India not infrequently met Indian Christians (usually in rural parts) who insisted upon the removal of one's footwear before entering a place of worship and would quote the command given to Moses (Exodus 3:5) and to Joshua (Joshua 5:15) in support.

We are under the necessity therefore of distinguishing between those commands of scripture that are to be obeyed literally everywhere and in all ages and those which are locally and culturally conditioned. With respect to the latter our responsibility as interpreters of scripture is to discern the Biblical principle lying behind the command or practice and then to insist that the principle be applied within the cultural context and local conditions in which we find ourselves. As examples of the universal commands of scripture we might adduce: "love one another" (John 13:34); "Go into all the world and preach the good news . . ." (Mark 16:15); "Be baptized, every one of you . . ." (Acts 2:38). But even with respect to the second of these three "universals" we shall need to exercise caution. It is universal in its application in the sense that the whole church throughout the whole of the age is under obligation to preach the gospel to the whole world. But it cannot possibly mean that every individual believer is to leave the place where he lives and works, and it certainly does not mean that every believer is to preach unless we are prepared to interpret "preach" (literally — "proclaim good news as an herald") as including every simple testimony borne by humble believers to their non-Christian neighbours.

As examples of the non-universal commandments we might adduce a great deal of the legislation (though not of course the Ten Commandments) laid down for Israel in the Pentateuch, which for example permitted polygamy, provided for the inflicting of 40 stripes save one, and the stoning of adulterers. From the New Testament

the command "you also should wash one another's feet"
(John 13:14); "Greet one another with a holy kiss"
(I Corinthians 16:20); and, "Use a little wine because of
your stomach" (I Timothy 5:23). In hot climates it
would be offensive to your hosts if you failed to remove
your shoes and to wash your feet or submit to having
them washed before sitting down, on the floor, to a meal.
In colder climes equal or even greater offence might be
caused if you removed your shoes in company.

The reference above to the legislation of the Pentateuch
reminds us that we are under the necessity of recognising
a certain dispensational pattern which will govern our
interpretation. In a very natural and proper reaction
against the extreme dispensationalism that is current in
some American Fundamentalist circles there are those
who go so far as to say that there is no dispensational
pattern at all in Biblical Theology. This is plainly absurd.
Without falling into the ultra-dispensationalist trap of
denying membership of the church to Abraham and
Moses and their fellow Old Testament believers we are
nevertheless bound to concede that God dealt with His
people in that age in ways which He no longer uses in
this. Much of the argument of the Hebrews epistle
depends upon this fact. With the arrival of Jesus Christ a
new age, the "last days", had begun. Should we not be
right in cautiously asserting that the apostolic age was
also in some respects unique and that some things may
have happened then which we should not expect to
happen now?

Acts 2 and 4 speak of a sort of primitive communism.
Is that example to be followed literally by all Christians
in all ages? A number of modern attempts to establish
a kind of Christian commune have ended disastrously.

The apostolic band was a unique provision for a transi-
tional period during which the church was planted
throughout the Roman Empire, securely established, and
finally left with a complete body of New Testament

revelation. Critics have thrown at us the cheap gibe that we believe ourselves, with the completed canon of scripture, to be better off than was the Apostle Paul. We do no such thing. All we are asserting is that for a brief period the infant church needed the guidance and direction of inspired apostolic men because they had no New Testament; whereas we, in our days, do not have the physical presence and face to face ministry of the apostles, nor do we need it, but we have their writings which are our infallible and completely reliable guide in all matters of faith and practice. Therefore we are under the necessity of enquiring if indeed all of Paul's instructions as to the regularising of charismatic manifestations in Corinth are appropriate in their literal sense to our church situation today? And whether the forwardness of a women's lib group in immoral Corinth really does supply us with detailed rules that are to govern the manner of women's attire to the end of time?

Is Deuteronomy 22:5 relevant to our contemporary situation and if so in what way? We sometimes fall into error because of our naivety or simplicity. Especially, those of us who belong to an earlier generation and were brought up in comparatively sheltered circumstances find it difficult to understand how vile was the life style of the inhabitants of Canaan or how abominable was the life style of the inhabitants of the Graeco-Roman world in the first century of our era. Unhappily we are now being severely shaken out of our innocency as these abominations become more and more common in our contemporary society. Sometimes we need to be able at least to guess at some of these evils to be able correctly to interpret some of the prohibitions of the Mosaic legislation and some of the advice given by the Apostle Paul to the Corinthians. To think that Deuteronomy 22:5 is concerned with 20th century women in Britain wearing slacks or trouser suits is a little too simple. It is far more likely that it was a prohibition of transvestite behaviour,

that is a perverse addiction on the part of males to dress-
ing in women's clothing and vice versa, so acting for
immoral purposes. Moreover the fertility cults connected
with the baal worship of Canaan probably included some
such conduct as do some forms of village Hinduism to this
very day in India.

So to sum up on this issue: "While this law in its original
setting has no direct implication for modern life, there
are some indirect implications. There are positive values
in preserving the difference between the sexes in matters
of dress . . ."² We have a perfect right to feel some dis-
taste for modern dress trends amongst women (and
amongst men!) but it would be unwise, uncharitable and
probably unscriptural to condemn the innocent wearing
of trouser suits by women as being "an abomination unto
the Lord" on the basis of Deuteronomy 22:5.

But before leaving this subject we must take serious
notice of the warning conveyed in the protest: "If we
say, 'Well, this or that just applied to the local situation',
we can dispense with large parts of scripture ... "
We must admit that the principle of *interpreting within
cultural context* is open to abuse and is liable to be applied
in a highly subjective manner. We must be aware of this
and on our guard. For example, many of the arguments
used above (and, we think, used properly) are now being
made to subserve the interests of those who are bent
upon ordaining women. But over and above any purely
cultural and local reasons that there may have been for
Paul's ban upon women intruding into the teaching office
and usurping authority there are clearly enunciated theological reasons going back to the very beginning of the
history of the human race and taking into account the
differing temperamental structures of the sexes. This
ban is, for these reasons, not culturally conditioned but
valid for all women in all ages. May God give us wisdom
to distinguish things that differ.

While grateful for all the light that streams upon the sacred page from a knowledge of the historical and cultural context within which the various Bible writers did their work we need to exercise much caution. We may well be astonished sometimes at the self-assurance with which, looking back through the mists of 2,000 years, some experts claim to understand the context in which the parables were uttered and the epistles written.

We must beware of being too much influenced by our own culture. If contemporary opinion in the world around us leans in a certain direction it is all too likely that such views will rub off on churches and their leaders. In the history of theology its moods frequently reflect with all too much fidelity those of secular society!

13.
A final caution

This book began with four basic rules. It is possible that some, having read thus far, may have gained the impression that understanding the Bible is merely a matter of applying the rules in a somewhat mechanical fashion. Let us be on our guard against the idea that correct rules of interpretation are all-sufficient, a kind of evangelical rationalism. We need the internal testimony of the Holy Spirit to convince us of the truth of Scripture so that we bow to the Lordship of Jesus Christ and accept the truth as from the mouth of God.

Scripture's ultimate author, the Holy Spirit, leads and enlightens the humble reader and so interprets the Word in our minds and our hearts. So whenever you take up the Book ask for the Holy Spirit's aid: "Open my eyes that I may see ... " However this perfectly proper dependence upon the work of the Spirit must not be turned into an excuse for laziness or the neglect of any help that may come our way. The Spirit's ministry is not opposed to our becoming acquainted with rules that govern the right interpretation of Scripture nor opposed to our using such rules. But through and beyond the rules and their use may the Word penetrate our minds and our affections producing obedience, love and joy so that we heed the warnings, believe the promises and become conformed to Christ. That is the work of the Holy Spirit.

Notes

Chapter 1

1. J. D. Douglas and others, eds., *The New Bible Dictionary* (London: Inter-Varsity Press, 1972).
2. Robert Young, *Analytical Concordance to the Bible* (London: Lutterworth Press, 1966).
3. James Strong, *The Exhaustive Concordance to the Bible* (London: Hodder and Stoughton, 1896).
4. A. Cruden, *Cruden's Complete Concordance* (London: Religious Tract Society, 1930).

Chapter 2

1. Brian H. Edwards, *Nothing but the Truth* (Welwyn, Herts.: Evangelical Press, 1978), p. 149.
2. *Ibid.*, plate VII (between pp. 114 & 115).
3. *Ibid.*, plate VIII (between pp. 114 & 115).
4. William Hendriksen, *A Commentary on the Gospel of John* (London: The Banner of Truth Trust, 1959), Vol. II, p. 24.
5. G. Campbell Morgan, *The Gospel According to John* (London: Marshall, Morgan and Scott, 1933), pp. 164–165.
6. H. C. G. Moule, *The Epistle to the Romans* (London: Hodder and Stoughton, 1896), pp. 140–141.
7. B. Metzger, *A Textual Commentary on the Greek New Testament* (London: United Bible Society, 1971), p. 511.

Chapter 3

1. D. Martyn Lloyd-Jones, *Romans: An Exposition of Chapter 5: Assurance* (London: The Banner of Truth Trust, 1971), pp. 184–187.
2. *Ibid.*, p. 6.

Chapter 4

1. For a detailed discussion of these matters see: Donald Guthrie, *New Testament Introduction* (London: Tyndale Press, 1970), and A. Cole, *Galatians* (London: Tyndale Press, 1965).
2. For a detailed treatment of these passages and of this subject see: W. J. Chantry, *Today's Gospel: Authentic or Synthetic* (London: The Banner of Truth Trust, 1970).
3. *The Analytical Greek Lexicon* (London: Samuel Bagster and Sons Ltd., 1977).
4. D. Martyn Lloyd-Jones, *Romans: An Exposition of Chapter 8:17–39: The Final Perseverance of the Saints* (Edinburgh: The Banner of Truth Trust, 1975), pp. 294–296.
5. cf. David Brown, quoted by Geoffrey B. Wilson, *I Corinthians* (London: The Banner of Truth Trust, 1971), pp. 140–141.

Chapter 5

1. See H. K. Moulton, *Challenge of the Concordance* (London: Samuel Bagster and Sons Ltd., 1977).
2. Geoffrey B. Wilson, *op. cit.*, p. 170.
3. L. Boettner, *Roman Catholicism* (London: The Banner of Truth Trust, 1966), p. 236.
4. *Ibid.*, pp. 142–143.

Chapter 6

1. *Chambers XX Century Dictionary* (London: W. & R. Chambers, 1962).
2. J. C. Nesfield, *Manual of English Grammar and Composition* (London: Macmillan and Co. Ltd., 1924), pp. 231–232.
3. J. C. Ryle, *Expository Thoughts on the Gospel of St. Luke* (London: Hodder and Stoughton, 1858), Vol. I, p. 343.
4. See the note in *The Scofield Bible* on Matthew 13:33, and G. Campbell Morgan, *Parables and Metaphors of our Lord* (London: Marshall, Morgan and Scott Ltd., 1943), pp. 51–56.
5. L. Berkhof, *Systematic Theology* (London: The Banner of Truth Trust, 1959), p. 66.

Chapter 7

1. J. C. Ryle, *op. cit.*, pp. 381–383.
2. William Hendriksen, *op. cit.*, pp. 293–317.

Chapter 8

1. J. Angus, *The Bible Handbook* (London: Religious Tract Society, 1904), pp. 224–225.
2. *Ibid.*, p. 225 (footnote).
3. *Ibid.*, pp. 226–227.

Chapter 11

1. These remarks consist, for the most part, of a conflation of material from J. Angus, *The Bible Handbook,* pp. 558–562, and C. S. Lewis, *Reflections on the Psalms* (London: Geoffrey Bles Ltd., 1958), pp. 3–5. For those with *The Scofield Bible,* there is an admirably brief and helpful introduction to the Poetical Books. Beware, however, of Scofield's quite unwarranted limitation of the Poetical Books. Angus wrote, "The writings of the prophets are for the most part in poetical form" (*op. cit.*, p. 558).
2. D. Kidner, *Psalms 1–72*, and *Psalms 73–150. Tyndale O.T. Commentaries.* (London: Inter-Varsity Press, 1973). D. Kidner, *Proverbs. Tyndale O.T. Commentaries.* (London: Inter-Varsity Press, 1968).
3. D. Kidner, *Psalms 73–150*, p. 345 (footnote).
4. *Ibid.*, p. 351 (footnote 1).

Chapter 12

1. Brian H. Edwards, *op. cit.*, pp. 128–131.
2. J. A. Thompson, *Deuteronomy. Tyndale O.T. Commentaries.* (London: Inter-Varsity Press, 1974).

Chapter 13

1. James Packer, *Scripture and Truth* pp. 347-348 (I.V.P. 1983)

Select bibliography

Angus, Joseph. *The Bible Handbook.* Religious Tract Society, London, 1904.

Berkhof, Louis. *Principles of Biblical Interpretation.* Evangelical Press, Welwyn, Herts., 1973.

Edwards, Brian H. *Nothing But The Truth.* Evangelical Press, Welwyn, Herts., 1978.

Pink, Arthur W. *Interpretation of the Scriptures.* Baker Book House, Grand Rapids, Michigan, 1977.

Sterrett, T. Norton. *How to Understand Your Bible.* Gospel Literature Service, Bombay, 1973.

Stibbs, Alan M. *Expounding God's Word.* Inter-Varsity Press, London, 1970.

Scripture Index